Contents

Preface to the English Edition

You have just opened the pages of an extraordinary document. It sheds a piercing light into the most obscured, most hidden, most forgotten corner of the crime of our century, the Holocaust. It is the largely unknown story of the wholesale slaughter of close to 400,000 Jews by the wartime Romanian government and the fascists of that country. Without this book, the story of the Holocaust is incomplete.

It is not a coincidence that this story has remained hidden for so long. Ever since the war and to this day, all the Romanian governments and most of the country's historians were united in a tacit conspiracy to deny, to obscure, to hide the truth about Romania's contribution to the Holocaust. And for good reasons, as that truth is abominable.

Romania has had the distinction of completing its own indigenous Holocaust, without much prodding from their German allies. In fact, as evidenced by this volume, mass butchering of Romania's Jews started well before the *Endloesung* was unleashed on the Jews of Germany and of the countries under German occupation.

No German prodding was needed as the methods of the slaughtering reached such incredible level of savagery that sometimes even German authorities felt compelled the protest the barbarism. Think about it. What it could take during the war to have Nazi German officials to protest the mistreatment of Jews.

In recent years if became fashionable in certain extreme right-wing circles to deny that the Holocaust ever took place. There are "experts" around the globe who spend a great deal of time and effort on denying the undeniable. In some countries such propaganda violates the law, in others its practitioners are simply dismissed as crackpots.

What we witness in this case is a monstrous, and so far largely successful, attempt of official Holocaust denial. The four volumes of this book were published in Bucharest between 1946 and 1948. Shortly after publication the Romanian authorities confiscated every available volume and fed them to the pulp mills. Romanian agents since have stolen and destroyed even most of those copies that found their way into foreign libraries. This book, until now, was practically unavailable for the outside world.

In this enforced silence carried on the official Romanian propaganda with perfect continuity through half a century. What this propaganda aided by Romanian "historians", has trumpeted around the world was their peculiar version of World War II history in which Romania was the only country under German influence or occupation that largely spared the Jewish population under its jurisdiction. This book shows the opposite to be true. If there was any distinction, it lay in Romania's preceding and occasionally surpassing Nazi Germany's brutality. What they lacked in the cold calculation of the diabolically systematic German death machine, the Romanians made up in the sheer savagery of their human slaughterhouses, the mass rapes of their victims wives and daughters, or the burning alive of 20,000 of Odessa's Jews.

The American reader might respond with incredulity to the horrors described here if the Serbian atrocities in Bosnia and Kosovo would not be so recent. One should be reminded that both the Serbians and the Romanians and their Southern neighbors had to endure 500 years of brutal oppression under the Ottoman empire while the rest of Europe has experienced the Renaissance, Enlightenment and Reformation. What happened in Srebrenica in July 1995 is not much different from what has happened in Iasi in June 1941.

Even before the reign of Vlad the Impaler, Romanian history was studded with unusually barbaric behavior. Twenty years before the Holocaust in Romania U. S. Major General Harry Hill Bandholtz, American Representative to the Inter-Allied Military Mission in Hungary—supervising the Romanian occupation of Eastern Hungary in 1919—wrote these in his diary[1]: "It is simply impossible to conceive such national depravity as those miserable "Latins" of Southeast Europe are displaying".... "Personally I

---

1   H. H. Bandholtz: *An Undiplomatic Diary.* ISBN 0-9665734-6-3

came here rather inclined to condone or extenuate much of the Roumanian procedure, but their outrageous conduct in violation of all international law, decency, and humane considerations, has made me become an advocate of the Hungarian cause." Bandholtz—who was Provost Marshal General of the American Expeditionary Force in Europe—wrote to British Foreign Secretary Earl Curzon: "Every effort humanly possible has been made by an Inter-Allied Military Mission, with the patience of a setting hen on a nest of china eggs, to coax Roumanian Headquarters into carrying out the expressed wishes of the Supreme Council or into keeping any of its solemn promises[2]. The goodwill was one-sided with a vengeance. Judging from the Roumanian occupation of Hungary, our little Latin Allies have the refined loot appetite of a Mississippi River catfish, the chivalrous instincts of a young cuckoo, and the same hankering for truth that a seasick passenger has for pork and beans."[3]

This is not an easy book to read and not only because of its horrendous content. Matatias Carp was no great writer and made no pretension of being one. Although at the time of publication he was the General Secretary of the Association of Romanian Jews, he stated in his own foreword that he wrote this book as a simple archivist, a chronicler of the sufferings of Romania's Jews. "I wrote this book of blood and tears with blood and tears..." he states elsewhere.

His deed has been of enormous significance. What he did was to bear witness in the real biblical sense. His prose may be simple, the marshaling of his data awkward, but he has recorded, for us all that was to be recorded, and all good men and women dedicated to remembrance as one way of preventing new holocausts will remain in Matatias Carp's debt forever.

2   British diplomat turned author, Lt. Col. Charles à Court Repington expressed an identical opinion when he wrote in his book: *After the War, a Diary*; Houghton-Miffin, 1922: "Roumanians are not remarkable for keeping promises or appointments". (fn. page 327). A splendid British understatement.

3   Ibid. Bandholtz: "The Rattigan Correspondence".

The original work comprises four volumes. The first one describes the anti-Semitic pogroms by the Iron Guard, a fascist Romanian organization trained in part by the Gestapo. The Iron Guard originally started as an extreme right-wing student movement but is soon grew into an SA type paramilitary terror gang. After Romania's wartime dictator Ion Antonescu took power in September 1940, the Iron Guard was unleashed on the political opposition and especially on the Jewish population of the country. During the following month thousands of Jewish homes and businesses were looted and destroyed, thousands of Jews tortured and killed in a whole series of the most brutal pogroms. The carnage was ended, temporarily, only by the suppression of the Iron Guard itself by Marshal Antonescu, not for their unspeakable crimes, of course, but because by that time the Iron Guard became a rival of the dictator himself. Another apt parallel with the ultimate fate of the German SA.

The second volume deals with the mass murder of the Jewish population in and around the Romanian town of Iasi. These events took place after Romania entered the war against the Soviet Union on the side of Nazi Germany in June, 1941. Iasi was a town with a large Jewish community in close proximity to the Soviet front. In this instance the Jews served—as so often in their tragic history—as scapegoats. Scapegoats for any failure or the Romanian army against the Soviets, for the evacuation of Bessarabia due to a Soviet ultimatum, for any successful Soviet attack or bombing raid. During the next few weeks tens of thousands of Jews were killed and deported. "Deported" meaning not some semi-orderly transfer, but methods that in themselves amounted to a way of mass killing. Very few of these "deportees" had a chance to reach any kind of destination.

The third volume is a chronicle of similar mass killings on territories that were temporarily occupied by Romania during the war, including Transnistria, Bukovina, Bessarabia and the Black Sea port of Odessa. The Jews of Bessarabia, the strongly anti-Semitic region that became part of Romania in 1918, died by the tens of thousands in such interment camps as Edineti, in death marches and ghettos. In Bukovina, more than 100 communities were uprooted and driven eastward. Most of the atrocities were committed in Transnistria, a territorial unit unfamiliar to most students of history of geography. This was an artificial province declared by Ion Antonescu, and carved out of Ukrainian territory between the rivers Dnyester (Romanian: Nistru) and Bug. It was possessed by Romania for 2 years and 7 months, plenty of time for the Romanians to butcher over 200,000 Jews there.

The above mentioned three volumes by Matatias Carp are included in the present edition. The fourth volume is omitted for the following reasons: This volume described the deportation of the Jews of Northern Transylvania in 1944. This however was not done under Romanian jurisdiction. The Second Vienna Arbitration of August, 1940 returned the Northern half of Transylvania—awarded to Romania as a result of World War I—to Hungary. After Germany occupied Hungary in March, 1944. Eichmann was dispatched to Hungary to administer the deportation of Hungarian Jewry, largely spared until that time.

Eichmann found plenty of Hungarian accomplices, parts of the gendarmerie, and Hungarian Nazi thugs. What is important, however, is that no Hungarian government since the war, or no Hungarian historian of any significance, ever tried to conceal from the world what happened to the Jews of Hungary, including, at that time, Northern Transylvania. The deportations started only after the German occupation of the country (March 19, 1944). There is no official Holocaust denial, no attempt to hide the complicity of some Hungarians in Eichmann's dirty work. In fact, the Hungarian Holocaust is well documented historically and even in literature. Hundreds of Hungarian Nazi collaborators were convicted and executed after the war for their crimes. As this book is about that part of the Holocaust that is "attributed" to the fascist regime of Ion Antonescu, Carp's fourth volume has no place in it.

Since the first publication in 1946, Matatias Carp's *Holocaust in Romania* has all but lost relevance. Traditional Romanian chauvinism and xenophobia have since compelled hundreds of thousands of Germans, Jews, and Hungarians to leave their homeland, bringing about a sharp drop in the percentage of German, Jewish, and Hungarian minorities to the Romanian majority. Such turn of events would be to the liking of Ion Antonescu, whose spirit seems to roam Romania's political establishment these days. Indeed, the fascist dictator and "Marshal" has been rehabilitated by Romanian Parliament; streets in Romanian towns have recently been renamed after him. With his statue erected in Slobozia, it was for the first time in post-war history that a war criminal and mass murderer should have been honored with a monument in a "democracy". This happened

October 22, 1993, with the assistance of Romanian government officials and members of parliament.

The revival of the Antonescu cult in today's Romania and the resurgence of institutionalized anti-Semitism only make the re-publication of Carp's book more timely. The weekly *Romania Mare* and the daily *Europe* regularly incite anti-Semitic feelings; such openly xenophobic groups as those called "Pro Bessarabia and Bukovina Cultural Association" and "League for Marshal Antonescu" unfortunately have political room in ultra-nationalist Romania to organize. By lack of attention, the free world may allow old mistakes to be repeated.

Romania must come clean on the events of its past and admit its profound guilt. Acknowledging guilt would lead to an awareness of the rights and wrongs of today as well. Such awareness, in turn, would provide a solid base for the aspirations of Romania's true democrats. The rule of true democracy would be a minimum requirement for a country knocking on the door of NATO and of the European Union.

Andrew L. Simon
Professor Emeritus
The University of Akron
March, 2000

Introduction

by Dr. Alexandru Safran, Chief Rabbi of the Romanian Jewish Congregation

Bucharest, January 21, 1946

Memory plays a major role in the life of man. According to a 17th century psychologist, its importance is so great that, "its absence would render most of our other capabilities useless".

The role of memory is equally important in the life of communities. Even though the transfer of every code from the memory of individuals to the level of collective psychology to the required extent may be impossible, we have ample opportunity to observe that the function of remembering—which is in fact much more than static memory—must be determined not only by psychological intentions but also by moral will. In the case of collective memory, we must also consider this moral obligation while practicing the ability to remember. It is this which also distinguishes collective memory from the transitoriness of individual memory. When a nation, or even mankind, collectively acts on the stage of history, with the help of the strength provided by remembering, it should serve this moral obligation. According to the Jewish religion, the divine spirit is omnipresent in history, and manifests itself in invincible moral laws, which place primary importance on the function of remembering. Jewish moral codes originate from the compelling necessity to remember. As individuals, we must keep a record of our lives, their events and accomplishments; these, however, do not remain as isolated frames but join the living images which keep our moral consciousness awake, and spur us on towards moral responsibility. From the beginning, the bible taught us, as a nation, to remember and not to forget:

"Remember the days of the past, think of the years of bygone peoples!" We are forced to remember, and never forget the sorrows inflicted upon us by the sons of Amalek a long time ago: "Remember how Amalek treated you on your journey to Egypt... do not forget this!" This episode serves as an historical lesson for us. The bible, while telling us this parable (...), gives us an opportunity to pass judgment, and to control conscience and reckoning.

The ability to remember is at the essence of our Jewish existence. It is not by accident that a Jewish physiologist, Richard Semon, attempted to prove that memory is not only a psychic gift, but that it is also possessed by living organisms. The characteristic of the protoplasm, the living cell, its ability to recognize, record and return impressions, was first called "Mneme" (memory in Greek) by Semon.

We can state, not only from the points of view of psychology, but also from physiology: the impressions we have received during centuries of sufferings, are ingrained in our psyche. These are often referred to in our Books of Remembrance, which contain useful teachings for us, and strict moral lessons for others.

At the end of the World War I, in 1919, Jewish thinkers, Nathan Birnbaum and Hugo Hermann, wrote a book on the sufferings of the Jews during the time of the Crusades. On the first page of the collection, the authors aptly cited the prophet Isaiah, ("and there was a great massacre in Edom's country..."), and the pious psalmodist, (Lord, remember the sons of Edom).

"Remember!"—indeed, this is the recurring motif of our history. Our history is the history of the spirituality and martyrdom which struggled for the great moral commandments, which were given first by us to mankind, and which we continuously state with the stubbornness of our religion.

Nathan Birnbaum and Hugo Hermann vividly present the suffering of Jews during World War I. With the help of the kaleidoscope of the Middle Ages, they describe the ideals, and claim that that era was the worst of all times.

All the past sufferings of Israel pale into insignificance when compared to the martyrdom Jewish peopled suffered during World War II. The prophecy of Talmud was fulfilled concerning the era before the Messiah, "the sufferings to come will be so great that you will forget the previous ones.

It is enough to skim through "Remember!"—how Jewish this title is—written by the Soviet-Jewish writer, Ilja Ehrenburg to realize that: the fragments describing Jewish martyrdom overshadow the flames of mediaeval auto-da-fes.

We must study the book written by Mr. Matatias Carp to be able to estimate the true pre-messianistic extent of Jewish sufferings. This book was written with "blood and tears". This profound compilation was saved in spite of the dangers. "The Black Book of the Sufferings of Romanian Jews" is a memorial commanding respect. It was erected with reverence in memory of the martyrs of Israel by the "Life General Secretary of the Sufferings of Romanian Jews". Mr. Matatias Carp lived through each moment of the moving reality of which his book speaks.

He deserves our gratitude for this.

The moral duty undertaken by the author in writing this book is accomplished if the book itself does nothing else but contribute to the respect of one simple commandment from the Mountain Zion: "Thou shalt not kill!" What else could the commandment be—asks Horia Carp, flag bearer of the struggle for justice—other than the first step towards recognizing the freedom of individuals! The commandment we received from the Mount of Zion was no more than an attempt at freedom.

Horia Carp, who rests in David's Castle, and who incidentally sang of this, the enlightened protector of freedom, can be satisfied in the knowledge that the pious zeal of her son has helped people listen with their inner moral strength to the commandment of Zion, "Thou shalt not kill!"

"Because the great commandment of the Jews, I repeat—says Horia Carp—was, "Thou shalt not kill!"

First, it must be normal for people to respect the lives of their brethren; only then can they then set out towards the peaks which bathe in the light of brotherly love.

Foreword to the Original Edition

Matatias Carp, General Secretary of the Association of Romanian Jews, January 1946

World War II has ended, but we still await the signing and stamping of the documents and "papers", and the laying to rest of the war with protocol celebrations. Nevertheless, the weapons have grown silent.

Conceited and criminal megalomania, which has been fighting the combined moral and intellectual powers of mankind for so long, now lies suppressed and in chains. Peace must be guaranteed, peoples yearn for freedom, and laws need to be modified. Life goes on, new events are rapidly unfolding, old ones are forgotten. During the last decade, however, much has happened; people must always be reminded of it, and it must never be forgotten.

The most painful of these is what happened to the Jews of Europe. In this war—apart from the peoples of the Soviet Union—it was the Jews who unselfishly placed themselves, their enthusiasm and their adoration at the disposal of their homeland and her high moral ideals. Theirs was the most moving blood sacrifice of history. We cannot find any other nation in the world who has sacrificed as many of her sons for her homeland, for justice, liberty and humanity as Jews have—even if we consider all the Allied Nations together.

And yet, the time has not come for the complete history of Jewish sufferings between 1933 and 1944 to be written.

Investigations, the gathering of data and research have been carried out throughout the world (the Anti-Fascist Committee in Moscow, the Black Book Committee in America, the Jewish World Federation, etc.), but so far no one has been brave enough to create a body of work that could be qualified as an historical piece.

If we quickly browsed through the archives and records of any of the aforementioned organizations (e.g. the Romanian Division of the Jewish World
Federation, which has collected a huge amount of information under the
encouragement of Kiva Ornstein, chairman of its Research Committee),
we could show how long it would take to compile a genuine scholarly work
containing the whole era of persecution and suffering. Only after years of
exhaustive research will teams of learned historians working under the
leadership of such outstanding personalities as Ilia Ehrenburg, Vasili
Grossmann (from the Anti-fascist Committee of Moscow), or Professor
Albert Einstein and Shalom Asch (from the American Black Book Committee) be able to present the history of Jewish suffering during the fascist
hegemony.

Science is slow. But we, who have experienced all the commotion, struggle
and sufferings of this era, need to learn everything that happened so as to
be able to form a conception of it which, although not holistic, is still suffi-
ciently lucid and close to the truth.

It is for this reason that I had already decided to write this book when I saw
and felt that our cause, which is an organic component of history, will
surely win out, since history will turn the scales in our favor, or perish if it
fails to do so.

I wrote this book of blood and tears with blood and tears to help my brethren find new incentives and objectives in life by remembering the pains experienced, and blows received, in the hope that they will discover means of
self-defense in the future, and so that the anger and disgust created by the
events presented herewith should make others acknowledge that they committed a great number of crimes against the members of our community.
They must provide comfort for the pain and go a long way towards easing
their conscience by accepting responsibility in the eyes of history.

I refrained from creating a work of literature. Do not look for stylistic
turns, metaphors, epic descriptions and vehicles for tragic pathos in this
book. I even tried to avoid the use of qualifying adjectives.

I also refrained from commending, judging, or defending one point of
view over another, and praising virtues or cursing sins. I did not write this
book in my capacity as the ex-General Secretary of the Union of Jewish Re-

ligious Communities, and neither as the present-day General Secretary of the Union of Romanian Jews, but as the archivist and cataloguer of Romanian Jewish suffering. I wrote this book for those who still do not know or do not want to believe what happened, and for those in the habit of forgetting too quickly.

Revenge is not on my mind. I am the son of a nation rich in culture and literature, and proud that the civilization which we gave mankind—which rocked the cradle of Moses, the prophets, Jesus Christ, Spinoza, Einstein and many more famous people—extinguished many base emotions inside us. Firstly, the passion for revenge.

I do not wish to take revenge on anyone; not for the sufferings, nor for the abuse which chased my father, whom I will not see again, to faraway places; not for the parents slaughtered at the bank of the Bug, whose two Transnistrian children, my children now—while not bodies of my body—are definitely souls of my soul. I do not seek revenge for the sufferings of any of my brethren living anywhere in the world.

However, I do want justice. I want holy justice to emerge from the good-will, minds and emotions of all civilized people; I want everybody who tortured and robbed others, or murdered innocent people to be punished. From its suppressed depths, I want to bring the pain of Jews to the surface; the pain which has so far been covered by trivialization. I want everyone to learn the truth, only the truth, and the whole truth.

For these reasons, I will momentarily lift the shroud which covers more than 400,000 dead bodies, and expose the robbery, which exceeded 1 billion dollars.

I have examined and authenticated every piece of data of the book; every statement is based on proof, most of which are irrefutable. This book consists of the statements, testimonies, and official communiques of the Union of Jewish Religious Communities and their official copies, which contain the signatures of all the members of the administrative hierarchy (from the Marshal to the lowest-ranking sergeant, or office head). There are photographs and other documents in this book (directives, reports, telexes, sales contracts, announcements reporting suicide, court-room decisions, etc.) as well as reports of investigations. The robberies and other ghastly acts of the Iron Guard were examined before the collapse of the system by two Christian lawyers, forced onto the Union of Jewish Religious Communities by "Iron Guard Aid". These robberies and other crimes during the period of the Iron Guard revolt were recorded by a committee of 30 Jewish lawyers, appointed by the Union of Jewish Religious Communities.

Part of the material on which this book is based was in the possession of the archives of the Union of Jewish Religious Communities. The only existing documents are the ones I managed to save before the Central Office of Romanian Jews was founded. The other part of the collection was thrown into a corner of a cellar, where, after August 23, 1945, I could not find anything other than a pile of rotting paper.

Certain directives were checked and completed with the help of the results of an investigation organized by the Romanian Department of the Investigating Committee of the Jewish World Federation, who also facilitated the publication of this book.

I had intended to organize the material into four volumes as follows:

> Volume 1: The Iron Guards and the Iron Guard Revolt
> Volume 2: The Antonescu Government and the War
> Volume 3: The Transnistrian Tragedy
> Volume 4: Northern Transylvania

The original intention was that the book should contain all the documents on which it is based. However, this would require 10-12 volumes, which is not feasible at present. Perhaps, this will be a task for the future. [Later the author modified his original plan, and the volumes were published under different titles. - Ed.]

The Black Book of the suffering of Romanian Jews is exclusively my personal work, and I accept responsibility for its contents. The gathering of data began in June 1940, and I started to organize the material in the spring of 1943 with the help of my only colleague, my wife, with whom I shared the work, the pain and the fear of persecution.

Part 1. The Iron Guard

The History of Anti-Semitic Persecution in Romania, 1940-1944

The sweeping persecution and terror wreaked on the Jewish population within the borders of Romania was as violent and devastating as that of the other countries under Nazi power or influence. The holocaust in Romania differed only in details of modus operandi and absolute and relative numbers of victims compared to countries where the Nazi persecution manifested itself in the most horrifying ways (Ukraine, Belarus, Poland, Hungary and Germany). The Romanian massacres lacked technological and scientific organization: there were neither gas chambers nor crematoriums to dispose of the bodies; the hair, teeth and fat of the victims were not utilized for industrial purposes. Romanian fascism employed its own unique methods of extermination, which differed from the classic ones known since the invention of rope and gunpowder. Here, people were beaten until they lost all their strength and succumbed; they were suffocated in carriages with sealed ventilating holes; certain victims were sold, (the selected ones were shot out of marching columns so that their clothing could be sold); Jews were cut into pieces so that the axles of carts could be smeared with their blood; the list of crimes continues.

Considering the many historical examples of thievery, Romania, above all other nations and eras, can boast of the most terrible acts of pillaging.

During the period in question, Jewish property, which had been rendered almost non existent, was at the disposal of all those who desired it, from the Romanian state to the pettiest thief. The criminals plundered, both highwaymen and ministers—the latter using different methods—but both criminals. Charitable people were not above such acts either—Jews were robbed to harm them, and also to save them from harm. They were robbed so that they could be killed, killed so that they could be robbed, and robbed because they had already been murdered anyway.

The extent of persecution in Romania is reflected by two figures:

1. From among the Jewish inhabitants of Romania, which in 1940 was estimated to be 760,000, approx. 400,000 were killed. Approximately 260,000 of these can be put down on the Romanian government's account, for the rest—the inhabitants of Northern Transylvania—the Hungarian[1] government is responsible.

2. The damage caused to the Jewish population of Romania exceeds $ 1 billion.

Some Statistical Data on the Jewish Population:

According to the national census on December 29, 1930 Greater Romania's Jewish population was 756,930. This was the last official census taken before 1939. The data regarding Jews in this census did not change considerably during the next ten years, until June 1940. In the April 6, 1942 national census taken by the Antonescu government, citizens of Jewish ethnicity were registered in a separate column. The number of Jewish citizens was determined to be 441,293. In Bessarabia and Bucovina and in territories surrendered to the Soviet Union in June 1940, and occupied in the summer of 1941, no official census was taken, only an official count, which was carried out by Romanian civil and military authorities on September 1, 1941.

In Hungarian controlled Northern Transylvania the original Jewish population according to the 1930 census figures was 148,294. According to the January 31, 1941 census the number of Jewish citizens was 151,125. Deportation of Jewish citizens in Northern Transylvania started in the

---

1   Deportation of Jews in Hungary started only after the German occupation, March 19, 1944. Romania was never occupied by Germany. (Ed.)

summer of 1944. By September 1, 1945, 29,405 returned from German concentration camps. Apparently thousands of Jews were still alive who did not yet returned home. The above figures prove that up to 121,270 Jews in Northern-Transylvania were missing and may have been killed in Nazi concentration camps.

The remaining territories consisted of the Old Kingdom, South-Transylvania, Bucovina and Bessarabia. According to the 1930 census figures, the Jewish population of these territories totaled 607,790. On May 20, 1942 a special count of Jewish citizens were taken in Romania. Their number was found to be 292,149.

The decline of Jewish population in territories affected by mass deportation was as shown below:

	Dec. 29, 1930 census	April 6, 1942 census	May 20, 1942 census
Bessarabia	206,958	72,625	227
Bucovina	93,101	71,950	17,113
Dorohoi County	14,874	11,546	2,316

The above figures show that from September 6, 1940, when the Romanian fascist dictatorship seized power, to May 20, 1942, when the national census of inhabitants of Jewish origin was taken, the number of Jewish citizens living within the borders of what was then Romania (excluding Northern-Transylvania) had decreased by 315,641. It is also true that at that time (May 20, 1942), of the Jews deported to Transnistria in the autumn of 1941 and the first half of 1942, tens of thousands were still alive. Even though an official count was never taken, a report issued by the Ministry of the Interior dated November 1943[2] revealed that as of September 1, 1943 the number of survivors was 50,741. Several thousand died or were killed after this date, and it is for this reason that, upon re-occupying Transnistria in March 1944, the Red Army found only 40 - 45,000 Jewish deportees living there. (This figure is based on approximate estimates, and not on official data.) However, if we accept the figure for survivors (50,741) given by the Ministry of the Interior, it is clear that 264,900 of the Jewish citizens of Romania (excluding Northern-Transylvania) are unaccounted for, i.e. 43% of the then Jewish population.

It can be said that these figures do not reflect reality since those Jews who escaped at the beginning of the war are not counted in them. Even if this statement were true, it would not alter the tragedy of these numbers. But it is not true. Verified information proves that the figure for those who tried

2   The report can be found in the 1943 "Transnistria" section of the secret archives of the Ministry of the Interior. It is neither signed nor dated. It was compiled by the ex-Deputy Secretary of State, General C. Z. Vasiliu. Its contents show that it was destined for the President of the Council of Ministers in November 1943. Among other things it contains this unedited extract:

"In the framework of the measures of autumn 1941 aimed at cleansing Bessarabia and Bucovina, following the reoccupation of these territories by the Rumanian army, the transfer of Jewish elements to Transnistria for subsequent execution by military police forces has been ordered. It was only possible to calculate the number following the gradual reinstatement of Rumanian administrative authority, while German troops were in the process of surrendering the territories.

Based on data now in our possession, the number of evacuees in 1941 was the following:

From Bessarabia:	55,867
From Bucovina:	43,798
From Dorohoi Co. and town:	10,368
Total:	110,033

During 1941 and 1942 some of these died of infectious diseases, the result of a lack of medical care and preventative treatment in territories close to the front line; according to the count carried out on September 1, 1943 some 50,741 Jews remained alive, the greater proportion of these was transferred to Moghilev, Tulcin to save their lives by escaping is very small. In Chernovitz there were hundreds, in the area of Kishinev thousands, and about the same number in Southern Bessarabia, in the vicinity of Cetatea Alba. The case could not have been otherwise if we consider the speed of the German-Romanian attack. The offensive started near the river Prut on July 3, following the occupation of the town of Strojineti. Chernovitz, Vijnita, Herta, Noua Sulita and Edineti were occupied on July 5, Hotin on July 6, Balti on July 9, and Kishinev on July 17. A few days later the whole western bank of the Dniester was under their control.

The flood of those escaping was caught up in German-Romanian motorized troops. There are many documents which verify this fact. Among others report No. 1108 of Lieutenant-Colonel Jean Poitevin, the military judge of the III Romanian army, dated August 10, 1941 contains the following:

"I report that on August 9 of this year near Rascov, a group of about 2,000 Jews moving in the direction of the Ukraine arrived at the abutment of the Vadu Rascu bridge. These people were escaping together with the Soviet army. The Jews were collected from the district by the Romanian army, and were directed towards military court offices and their homes. The marching column, whose members were in a state of complete misery, was stopped on the eastern bank of the Dniester.

and Golta counties, and the rest to other counties.

The figures referring to the number of deported Jews do not seem exact. They are even contradicted by certain documents prepared during their deportation. The summarized report prepared by the Central Office of the Gendarmerie between December 15, 1941 and January 15, 1942, under the title "The Jewish issue," contains the following extract:

"So far 118,847 Jews have been taken across the Dniester to bring them, via Iampolon (35,276), Moghilev (55,913), Tiraspol (872), Rabnita (2,457) and Iasca (2,216), to the river Bug."

It must be emphasized that this "information" was gathered in January 1942, before the deportations of the same year, in which more than 12,000 people were dragged away.

I sent an officer to the scene accompanied by 20 Gendarmes to push them back to the Ukraine as far as possible.

I ordered the offices of military tribunals to send the Jews forwards, not backwards."

Telegraphic report No.602 dated August 17, 1941 from the Central Office of the Gendarmerie in Iasi, which was sent to the Military Tribunal Office, also referred to this issue:

"On the morning of August 17 the Germans took 12,500 Jews from Impel to Cosauti, from among those attempting to escape with the Red Army; these Jews were taken to a clearing near Cosauti where Gendarmes, frontier guards and 'paramilitaries' guarded them."

Of those who tried to save their lives by running away, only very few succeeded. Most of those went in the direction of Moscow, and the others went from Cetatea Alba to Odessa, and from there escaped by sea.

The above data also indicates that more than half of the victims— 166,497 people—died before September 1, 1941 or to be more precise, between the outbreak of the war June 22, 1941 and September 1, 1941, when the occupation of territories previously handed back in 1940 ended, and when those Jews still alive, were officially counted. The remaining figure of 100,000 approx. were either killed by the Iron Guard or during the pogrom in Iasi. They may have died on the roadside en route to concentration camps, or actually in the camps themselves due to misery, cold, hunger, disease and Romanian-German fascist brutality. /... /

An Outline of the Suffering of Romanian Jews

September 6, 1940 - August 23, 1944

I. Murders and Massacres

On June 29-30, 1941, at the Central Police Station, in streets, and in houses the police along with Romanian and German soldiers killed several thousand Jews in Iasi.[3] Of those who survived the bloodbath, 4,400 were directed to a concentration camp in Wallachia on board two trains. The ventilation holes of each cattle wagon were sealed, and 150-180 people were pushed inside. Carbide had been left inside the wagons. During the journey two-thirds of the evacuees died as a result of inhaling the poisonous vapor. The brutal torture of the previous day coupled with a lack of water had decreased their physical resistance.

In Podul Iloaiei 1,194 bodies were unloaded from the first train after a distance of 20 kms.., covered in 12 hours.[4]

From the second train in Tirgu Frumos (40 kms..) 650, in Mircesti (85 kms..) 327, in Sabaoan (95 kms..) 172, in Roman (110 kms..) 53, in Inotesti (370 kms..) 40 dead bodies[5], and in the last station in Calarasi-Ialomita (563 kms..) 25 dead bodies, 69 dying and 1,011 persons who were still alive were unloaded.[6] Of the latter, 128 died at the camp in Calaras.[7]

3   The exact figure has not been established. Based on the announcements of a minister (I. Hudila)—the first to visit Iasi after the armistice—of the Romanian government which came into being after 23 August 1944, it is clear that the combined number of victims of the Iasi pogrom and the death trains is more than 12,000.

As the Romanian and German units advanced between June 22 and July 30, 1941 in Bucovina and Bessarabia, almost the entire Jewish population living in villages was executed. In Noua Suliata 800 people were killed; in Herta 100 hostages were killed and buried in three mass-graves; in Ciudei the entire Jewish population was exterminated (approx. 500 people); in Vijnita 21; in Rostochi 140; in Edineti 500, in Vascauti 20; in Harbova all 10 Jews; in Banila pe Siret "only" a few were killed, but they were cut to pieces so that the axles of carts could be smeared with their blood; in Hlinita and Drosnita 90% of the Jewish population was killed; in Parlit 10 Jews were murdered under circumstances so horrifying that even the German army were shocked, and lodged a complaint[8] with the Romanian Chiefs of Staff; in Briceni and Lipcani the number of murdered could not be calculated; in Teura Noua 50 Jews were killed in circumstances that caused the German army to protest again[9]; in Cotman 10 Jews (including the rabbi); in Lipcauti 40 were killed; in Ceplauti the entire Jewish population of 180 was exterminated; in Zoniachie 139; in Rapujinet 37; in Marculesti first 18 (including the rabbi), and two days later 600 Jews were murdered.[10]

In the towns there large-scale mass-murders were performed with extreme brutality. In Storojineti, on the day of occupation (July 3), 300 Jews were killed, two days later 15 more; in Chernovitz on the day it was occupied July 6) more than 2,000 Jews were killed, a further 300 were shot dead two days later, as was the chief rabbi; in Hotin Jews lived on the outskirts, and

4   Report No.4457 of the Third Office of the Gendarmerie in Iasi—
     dated July 6—sent to the Central Superintendency of the Gen-
     darmerie.

5   Report No.1324 dated July 4, 1941, from the Gendarmerie Le-
     gion of Romania to the Central Superintendency of the Gendar-
     merie.

6   Minutes compiled by Sub-Lieutenant Triandaf Aurel, the com-
     mander of the train, and of the local civil and military authorities in
     Calarasi on July 6, 1941.

7   Ibid.

on the first day of the occupation of the town (July 7) almost every Jew was murdered (approx. 2,000 people). Massacres still continued in the town for three more days.

On July 17, in Kishinev, alongside the two roads on which the Romanian army forced its way into the town, more than 10,000 Jews were killed.

On July 11, in Balti, which had been occupied on June 9,10 Jewish hostages were shot dead by the Gestapo; on July 15 another 56, along with all the elders of the religious community; on July 16, 20 more hostages were murdered.

8   The protest was dated July 14, 1941, and signed by the General Chief of Staff of the XI German Army. It was forwarded by Rumanian General Headquarters to the judge of the military tribunal under order 1665/B of July 19, 1941.

The protest, which included the reports of witnesses and that of the German military secret police, also contains the following:

"The behavior of certain representatives of the Rumanian army, which have been indicated in the report, will diminish the respect of both the Rumanian and German armies in the eyes of public here and all over the world."

In spite of all this, the case was closed because upon examination (report No.258 of the Balti Gendarmerie Legion on August 14, 1941 sent to the Central Office of the Gendarmerie in Kishinev), it was concluded that nobody was found guilty and nobody could be held responsible.   Report No.223 of July 17, 1941.

9   The protest was dated July 11, 1941, and signed by the General Chief of Staff of the XI German Army. Rumanian General Headquarters forwarded it to the chief judge of the military tribunal under order 1411/B on July 17, 1941. Copies of the official report of a meeting of the German military secret police as well as statements taken at the scene were also included with the protest.

10   Report No.10952 of July 6, 1941 by the Gendarmerie Legion of Prahova to the Central Superintendency of the Gendarmerie

The above figures are examples only from areas where it was possible to carry out inspections. The number of murders was much higher.

One example gives a more exact picture of the truth. In Balti county, according to official statistics, the Jewish population was 31,916. After the Romanian and German armies had occupied the entire county, the chief military judge of the army informed General Headquarters on July 17, 1941 (24), that there were only 8,481 Jews left in the county, and that they had been gathered into three concentration camps. As the above-mentioned facts prove—based on the data of the official censuses and counts—166,497 Jewish men, women, children and elderly people had died in Bessarabia and Bucovina by September 1, 1941.

Even though a certain sense of order came about following the cessation of military operations, the killing and slaughtering of Jews continued.

On August 1, a German lieutenant and three soldiers selected 411 Jewish intellectuals from the ghetto in Kishinev and shot them 2 kms. from the town.[11]

On August 7 and 8,1941 a further 525 Jews were selected from the ghetto in Kishinev and taken to the railway station at Ghidighic. Only 200 returned. They claimed that the others had been killed.

On August 6, 1941 members of the Kishinev police division executed 200 Jews, and threw them into the river Dniester.[12]

On August 9, 1941 gendarmes from the Chilia Legion shot 451 Jews in the camp at Tataresti.[13]

11　Report No.2 of the committee established to examine contraventions in the ghetto in Kishinev. The members of the committee were General C. Nicolescu, General St. Stroe, Military Judge, L. Preotescu, Chairman of the High Court of Justice, Traian Niculescu, Attorney General, L. Paunescu, Senior Supervisor of the National Bank, and A. Madarjac, Military Judge.

From among the starving, exhausted Jewish marching columns, which wandered hither and thither under the command of the Northern Bessarabian authorities, many thousands were shot dead or drowned. In one such marching column, consisting of 25,000, which had been taken across the Dnyester to the Ukraine, and then back to Bessarabia, 4,000 died in three weeks.

A group consisting of 300 Jews, escorted by a sergeant and two gendarmes from Volcinet, was either shot into the water of the Dnyester, or drowned while crossing the river.[14]

In the concentration camps of Bessarabia, where Jews were rounded up before deportation (Secureni, Edineti, Vertujeni, Marculesti), several hundred died daily.[15]

Along the roads where deportees were escorted, several thousands died of exhaustion, illness, hunger and the cold weather. (September 1941 was the time of the camps in Bessarabia, October and November for those in Bucovina, Dorohoi county and the ghetto of Kishinev). In one of the marching columns, which had started from Edineti on the night of October 15 in a village called Corbu, 860 Jews froze to death, among them there were many women holding their children in their arms.

12   The report by telephone of the Central Office of the Gendarmerie in Kishinev (Colonel T. Meculescu) dated August 13, 1941 to the Highest Military Tribunal.

13   Ibid., and also the official report compiled by SS Untersturm- fuhrer Heinrich Frolich and Captain Vetu Gheorghe Ioan of the Gendarmerie Legion of Chilia-Noua on August 9, 1941, which indicates that the former forwarded the order for execution to the latter on behalf of General Antonescu, and the latter executed the order. Captain Vetu was later found guilty by the Court of Justice, not, however, because he had killed so many innocent people, but for committing petty crimes while carrying out his duties: he stole watches and rings.

A number of people were killed by the gendarmes who escorted the marching columns. Under the orders of the Romanian military authorities, those lagging behind were to be shot.[16] Certain Jews were sold to villagers. These were then shot dead so that the buyers could receive the clothes of the victims. During their first winter in Transnistria, approx. 50,000 of the Jews deported from Romania died of cold, hunger, exhaustion and infectious diseases (typhoid, petechial typhus, dysentery, etc.).

14   Report No.121239 of September 17, 1941 by the Military Judge of the III Army, Lieutenant-Colonel Jean Poitevitin, sent to the Highest Military Tribunal contained the results of examinations conducted by the Gendarmerie Legion of Soroca in connection with this massacre. The following remark appears in the report:

"September 2, 1941. The case of the 200 Jews shot dead near the Dniester was examined by General Topor, who later closed the case. Illegible signature m.p."

15   Statements by witnesses against war-criminals who were commanders of the Jewish concentration camps in Vertujeni and Marculesti, from the indictment of the People's Tribunal (Collection VII, No.23/945): From the testimony of Colonel Alexandru Constantinescu:

"The 21-23,000 Jews brought from Bucovina and Bessarabia by the Gendarmerie Legions could not be accommodated in the small town of Vertujeni. This was the cause of despicable overcrowding. We could not even guarantee all of them a place to rest. Women, children, girls, men, the ill and dying, a mixture of people confined in conditions impossible to describe, and worse still, without eating facilities. The result: the growing number of deaths." From the testimony of Dr. Epurescu Alexandru, a Lieutenant:

"These starving and ragged people brought from another forest camp were in terrible condition. The number of deaths increased."

From the evidence of witness Stefan Dragomirescu:

Most of them, however, were killed. Just a few examples: In Grozdovca, in October 1941 deported Jews were randomly executed in groups of ten every day by Romanian soldiers.

On December 19, 1941, the military judge of the Sargorod-Moghilev district caught a glimpse of six young Jews on the highway and ordered them shot. The execution took place in the village cemetery. The following day two more Jews were shot dead under the orders of the same judge, one because he was said to have stolen two kilos of sugar, the other because he had supposedly sold meat on the black-market.

"When I arrived at Marculesti, I found thousands of deportees kept in indescribable conditions. The corpses of deportees lay everywhere, cellars, ditches, and in yards."

16   The above cited report of the committee founded to examine contraventions committed in the ghetto of Kisinev, contains the following details:

"This special order was given to him by the Commander of the Hotin Legion, Major Dragulescu, who informed him that, on orders from General Headquarters, Jews who were unable to keep up with marching columns due to either illness or tiredness, were to be executed. He was consequently ordered to send one reenlisted non-commissioned officer on each route, two days before the start of every marching column, to dig a hole every ten kilometres large enough to accommodate 100 bodies with the help of the Gendarmerie stations located on the way. Those unable to march with the columns were to be shot dead and buried in these holes. The "premilitaries" from the villages on the route of evacuation were to help them dig the holes and bury those shot dead.

Lieutenant Rosca executed the given orders with precision, and as a result 500 Jews were shot dead on the Secureni.- Cosauti route.

The same method was used in the case of the marching columns following the Edineti-Cosauti route, where the executioner was the same Lieutenant Popovici under the commission of Lieutenant Rosca Augustin."

On March 9, 1942, German soldiers stationed in the villages of Mostovoi and Zavadovca took 772 Jews from the camp at Cihrin (Berezovca County) and shot them on the outskirts of the village.[17]

On March 16, 1942, a group of 16 German soldiers (the SS unit stationed in Nova Candelli village in Berezovca county) took 120 Jews from the camp in Catousca, and killed them by shooting them in the head at the edge of the village.[18]

On April 4, 1942, in Rabnita 48 Jewish deportees were executed on the command of the leader of the Gendarmerie Legion for stepping out of the ghetto.

Between May 27 and 30, 1942, on the collective farm in Suha-Verba (Berezovca county) German military police from Lichtenfeld killed 1,200 Jews.[19]

On September 29, 1942, in Rastadt (Berezovca County) an SS group, lead. by an officer, shot dead 598 deported Jews from Bucharest, and in their efforts to round the number off, 400 local Jews were also killed.[20]

17   Report No. 189 from the Gendarmerie Office in Transnistria (Colonel E. Brosteanu) on 16 June 1942 to the Central Superintendency of the Gendarmerie.

18   Report No.187 from the Gendarme Office in Transnistria (Colonel E. Brosteanu) on 24 March 1942 to the Head Office of the Gendarmerie.

19   Report No. 185 from the Gendarmerie Office in Transnistria (Colonel E. Brosteanu) on March25, 1942 to the Head Office of the Gendarmerie.

20   It seems that 16 out of these 598 deported Jews managed to escape with their lives. On the list of Jews belonging to this category - contained in report No.42411 of June 16, 1943 sent to the Ministry of the Interior by the Central Superintendency of the Gendarmerie—these 16 Jews were listed as "alive in Transnistria", while the other 582 were declared "missing".

On October 10, 1942, 80 children, 40 women and old persons were selected from the camp at Ciricov, taken to a nearby forest and shot dead.

On the same day in the Krasnopolsk camp 80 Jews were shot dead: women, children and old people.

On October 14, 1942, in the camp in Ga Gaisen 230 Jews—women, old people, children—were executed.

On October 16, 1942, an Oberfeldwebel with some German soldiers took 150 Jewish girls from the camp of Peciora, all of them were hurt, some were even raped. They were later taken to the woods between Bar and Vinita, where they were shot dead.

On November 6, 1942, 1,000 deported Jews were killed in Ga Gaisen camp.

On the same day almost all Jews deported to Brailov were slaughtered. Two hundred and fifty of them succeeded in escaping, but within a month they were captured and later shot dead on December 5.

On January 5, 1943, under the pretext that they had escaped from the ghetto, 72 Jews deported to Iampol were shot dead.

On March 16, 1943 in Rabnita prison 68 people were slaughtered from among the deported communists. All of them were Jews.

The above enumerated events are only randomly selected examples from the enormous amount of murders committed by the German and Romanian armies in Bucovina, Bessarabia and Transnistria.

II. Beatings, Abuse and Torture

Under the Iron Guard government, the Iron Guard police, Iron Guard units, and the Iron Guard Workers' Association were among the many groups which abused, tortured and terrorized thousands of Jews throughout the entire country.

People were beaten with clubs, iron bars, pizzles and other specially employed instruments of torture; victims were forced to lie on the floor or a table while four ogres beat them with wet rope working in unison like smiths forging iron "with four hammers"; people were beaten with glass, which broke on their bodies, and were then forced to lick the blood off the hands of their executioners or off the floor. They were fed with soap and if they objected, it was pushed down their throats with a pizzle. They were locked into fumigating chambers, and kept there until they suffocated or were scalded. People were forced to take laxatives in enormous quantities (100 grams of sodium-sulphate mixed with vinegar and petrol). They were kept inside for 70 hours to float in their own excrement. People were tied to "shame-poles", where children threw stones at them, and pulled their hair, etc.

Later a large number of Jews were beaten and tortured in details en route to labor service. The beatings were ordered by the highest ranking officers.[21]

Jews were also beaten in the Targu-Jiu concentration camp, in the camps and ghettos of Bessarabia and Bucovina, in marching columns, and on the trains which evacuated or deported them. Jews suffered acutely during evacuations by train, when 150 people were packed into every carriage. They were transported for six days in the heat of July, and were not allowed a drop f water. Occasionally the doors of the freight cars were opened, and

21   Extract from Directive No.55500, one of the General Directives of
      June 27, 1942, issued by the First Department of the General
      Chiefs of Staff, which controlled the labor service: "For minor mis-
      demeanors (arriving late for assembly, negligence, undisciplined
      behavior) committed by labor service troops, the commander
      shall use corporal punishment."

      Extract from the Directive of September 12, 1942 from the First
      Department of the General Chiefs of Staff, which "supplements
      and clarifies" law No.55500:

      "Mr. Marshall does not want to see this work halfheartedly carried
      out but to be taken very seriously. Consequently, severe forms of
      punishment were also ordered: there were regular beatings and
      people were deported to Transnistria."

water brought in buckets. However, the water was not for them to drink, it was poured on the tracks before the very eyes of the parched passengers.[22]

III. Plundering

From the first days of the fascist government until the final hours before the collapse of the regime, the Jewish citizens of Romania were robbed unremittingly on an unimaginable scale. Many people took part in these robberies from those of the lowest strata to the highest, including the authorities.

1. Robberies Committed by Members of the Iron Guard

Members of the Iron Guard committed large-scale and brutal looting. Acts of looting were carried out by individuals and organized bands with the support and encouragement of authorities whose duty in every civilized country is to safeguard the property and lives of its citizens. The main methods of robbery employed by the Iron Guard were the following:

(a) Iron Guard Aid: Through terror and torture, this supposedly charitable Iron Guard institution, robbed Jews of cash and goods worth hundreds of millions of lei. Such incidents were widespread in Piatra Neamt, Buhusi, Targu-Neamt, Iasi. In Bucharest the Lord Mayor's Office of the third "Albastru" district was especially renowned for this activity. Similar acts also occurred in Ploiesti, Targovite.

The institution, founded at the peak of the terror, had little difficulty in achieving its aim. The intimidated and broken Jews succumbed easily to the frightening clubs and revolvers pointed at them. All Iron Guard social

---

22 Report No.22088 of June 25, 1941 issued by the Police Headquarters in Bacau, a town which was granted municipal authority, justifies the use of police force by reporting that a woman from Daraban was made to get off the train because she went mad on the way to the concentration camp.

institutions were founded on Jewish wealth: Iron Guard cooperatives, Iron Guard eateries, Iron Guard shops, etc.

(b) The Confiscation of Business Premises and Shops: This operation, which started in October 1940, and continued until January 1941, was headed personally by the Deputy Executive President of the Council of Ministers, and overseen by the Ministry of the Interior. These measures affected the entire country, and their aim was to deprive Jews of their trade and property, both landed and industrial.[23]

Through fear and torture they succeeded in putting their hands on almost every Jewish business in Transylvania and Oltenia, except for Timiosara, and two firms in Craiova. Businesses were acquired for five to ten percent of their market value, and in ninety percent of cases this money was not even paid. Shops and many commercial and industrial firms were snatched up in Bucharest and other parts of the country (Turnu Ma Magurele, Constanta, Giurgiu, Slatina, Caesti, Urziceni, Calarasi, etc.) It is impossible to estimate the scale of these robberies. /.../

(c) Burglaries: While the above operations were in progress, another smaller-scale activity was also taking place to remove belongings from Jewish homes. Similar means of torture and fear were applied to rob Jewish flats. Everything was taken, down to the last chairs and pillows, not to mention substantial amounts of cash, large quantities of jewelry as well as art pieces and libraries.

(d) The Iron Guard Revolt: during the three days of the uprising, synagogues, Jewish institutions, businesses, and flats were robbed and set ablaze in Bucharest. /.../

23   According to General Petrovicescu, Minister of the Interior, this
      action was "a battle to buy up Jewish shops and real estate."

2. Robbing Evacuees

The Jewish citizens of the country, once removed from towns and villages were robbed. /.../ Carters and members of the Gendarmerie took all the valuables these poor people were able to carry. In many areas, such acts of looting were completed by locals with the blessing of the authorities. Everything was removed from uninhabited Jewish homes, even window frames and the tin from roofs. In some places, even tombstones were taken from Jewish cemeteries so that they could be used as steps at the entrances of houses.

At a later stage the state itself joined in this robbery by passing a law ordering an auction of evacuees' property, which was regarded as abandoned.

3. Robbing Deportees

The robbing of deportees, carried out with bestial rage and insatiable avarice by the authorities (National Centre for Romanianization, the National Bank of Romania, County Halls, City Halls, etc.), officials in charge of deportations (officers, police inspectors, Gendarmes, police constables, etc.) and the local Aryan citizens, was more serious and more destructive in its consequences.

Jews were robbed everywhere: when the occupying troops marched in, in concentration camps and ghettos, during the long and lonely wanderings of marching columns, while crossing the river Dnyester, and finally, in the camps and ghettos of Transnistria.

(a) Looting flats: /.../ What had been left behind by the occupying troops, was confiscated by the authorities since Jews were only allowed to take with them to the ghettos or camps as much as they could carry on their backs, and many times not even that. Aryan citizens were strictly forbidden to buy Jewish property. This crime was punishable by death.[24]

The leftovers of official plundering were removed at stations passed by Jewish deportees on their way towards "their land of endless Calvary". Most of them arrived there only "with what they were wearing"[25]

(b) Stealing cash, gold and jewelry: one of the decisions of the Romanian National Bank, with the consent of higher authorities, obliged Jewish deportees to deposit their cash (lei and foreign currency), gold and jewelry in the bank. In return they were given Soviet rubles or Reichkreditkassenschein marks, which had no coverage (and were only valid in occupied territories).[26]

Exchange rates were calculated arbitrarily and with hostility, and ridiculously small amounts were paid.

24   Directive No.38 of October 11, 1941, issued by General Corneliu Calotescu, Governor of Bucovina, is an instance of this.

25   Report No. 116 of October 31, 1941 referring to the crossing-place at Otac (without signature and issuing authority). It was addressed to the Military Judge of the army on November 2, 1941 and also contains the following extract:

"The information given by the local Gendarmerie makes it clear that gold was taken away from Jews by the kilo, and dollars as well as other valuables were confiscated from them. After they had crossed the river Dniester at Moghilev, their sacks were taken away together with the belongings they still had. All these were stocked in a large barn, and the Jews proceeded with the clothes they were wearing, and without money."

General Ion Topor, the Military Judge of the army, wrote this remark on the margin of the information report: "I think this report may be true". He ordered an investigation, which, naturally, did not produce any results.

26   In territories affected by mass-deportation, the cash of Jews underwent the following "transfiguration": in July 1940 Soviet administrative authorities obliged the citizens to exchange lei for rubles; 40 lei for 1 ruble.

In July 1941 the Romanian administrative authorities obliged the citizens to exchange rubles for lei; 1 ruble for 1 leu.

In October 1941 the Romanian National Bank obliged Jews to exchange lei for rubles; 40 lei for 1 ruble.

(c) Stealing aid sent to deportees: The authorities—acting on the orders of Ion Antonescu—for a long time forbade the sending of individual or collective aid, which could have eased the plight of deportees. In spite of the danger, on many occasions people attempted to send food, clothing, money or other items in secret. However, not even one hundredth of the parcels reached the addressees; either because of the ill-will of the "benevolent" people who undertook to transport them and later stole them, or due to especially alert guards, who confiscated all parcels discovered. /.../

4. Pay-offs and Profiteering

The extortion of pay-offs and "gratuity" payments was a widely used means of acquiring Jewish wealth. People, however loose their contact with offices or organizations dealing with Jews or Jewish property was, found themselves in a position to make the best use of their situation for personal gain. Jews had to pay smaller or larger sums, amounting as a whole to billions of lei, in order to obtain various services. However, in most cases they had to pay to prevent, mitigate or avoid suffering. Money was taken from Jews by ministers, senior secretaries, officers of higher and lower ranks, court judges and members of the administration, both senior and junior. The amounts paid were appallingly high. The sum asked for exemption from work for a couple of days could reach as high as 50,000 lei. Sometimes 200,000 lei was asked for permission to travel from one town to another; if someone wanted to move away because of their fear of bomb attacks, the amount of money required for permission was occasionally set at one million lei. For a booklet, certifying the holders' exemption from obligatory work, in most cases 500,000 lei was paid; the price for bringing home families deported to Transnistria was sometimes as high as 5 million lei.

Later in Transnistria rubles were exchanged for German marks (Reichskassenschein); I mark for 60 rubles. In this way, if a Jew had had 1 million lei in savings on July 1, 1940, he received 25,000 rubles for it, and in July 1941 he was paid 25,000 lei for it, and for this amount he received 600 rubles in October 1941, and later for the same amount he received 10 RKKS marks, which was equal to the price of a loaf of bread.

There were, however, many instances when money was acquired, and promises remained unfulfilled.

5. Gruesome Robberies

The bodies of Jews killed on the first night of the Iron Guard revolt, and of those who died in the overcrowded freight cars of Iasi, or perished on the roads of Transnistria were robbed. Clothing was pulled off their corpses, and their golden teeth were broken out of their mouths.[27]

Occasionally one or two Jews were taken out of a marching column of deportees. They were sold for 2-3000 lei to villagers, who killed them for their clothing and personal belongings.[28]

27   The report of the committee established to investigate the irregularities which took place in the ghetto of Kishinev contains the following regarding this issue:

"The peasants living next to the route, upon learning of the planned measures regarding the digging of holes and the subsequent burials, waited in hiding alongside the road, among the corn-fields and in other different hiding places for the execution to be carried out so that they could throw themselves on the bodies to rob them." /.../

28   Although the Bessarabian deportations started in September, and those in Bucovina at the beginning of October, the sending of aid was only permitted on December 10 (C.B.B.T. document No.259 of the Presidium of the Council of Ministers to the Union of Jewish Religious Communities). The actual sending of aid became possible, however, only after February 10, 1942, when document No.04687 of February 5, 1942 of the Governorship of Transnistria reached the Central Office of the Romanian Jews; this document contained the exact orders regarding the sending of aid. By this time, however, in Transnistria almost 50,000 Jews had died of cold, hunger, starvation, disease and misery.

IV. Expropriation Acts

Under provisions laid down in the expropriation act, the following became the property of the state without any compensation:

(a) The property of Jews living in the provinces, i.e. plough-land, hayfields, grazing ground, uncultivated areas, lakes, vineyards, country-mansions, parks, orchards, livestock- and poultry-breeding houses, bee-keeping farms, vegetable-gardens, flower gardens as well as all animate and inanimate items of inventory, and supplies of grain and feedstuffs;

(b) Forests under Jewish ownership, together with buildings, equipment, tools and rail-tracks; all types of mills, even those used in towns; country oil-mills and country textile mills along with the adjoining land, animate or inanimate items of inventory, finished products and raw materials; distilleries, even if they happened to be in towns, with their land, buildings, equipment, animate or inanimate items of inventory, finished products and raw materials; timber mills including land, buildings, equipment, etc.;

(c) Ships, boats and other floating vessels;

(d) Real estate in towns, including adjoining land;

(e) Film studios and printing plants

(f) Livestock-breeding farms, bakeries, equipment for pastry production; any type of secondary industrial establishments belonging to mills; distillation plants, first and second class distilleries and refineries, boilers of all categories for spirit distillation; industrial firms producing medicine and medicinal raw materials; rights to subsoil utilization in areas where the topsoil was Jewish property; timber—in forests, stock or under transportation—owned by either the owner of the forest or the exploiter; animate or inanimate items of inventory related to the above-mentioned, and assets, equipment, rail-tracks, etc.;

(g) Shares in travel and tourist businesses owned by Jews;

(h) Directives were issued to facilitate the reclaiming of mortgages taken out on Jewish-owned real estate long before they were due;

(i) Goods, a large number of temples, synagogues and cemeteries owned by Jewish religious communities;

(j) All industrial and commercial businesses owned by Jews in Bessarabia and Bucovina

V. Confiscation

Confiscated by force of law or administrative measures:

-medical equipment owned by hospitals and private doctors (especially dentists and radiologists);
-radio equipment;
- bicycles;
-skis and ski equipment;
-the batteries, telescopes and cameras in some villages;
-the commercial and industrial businesses of owners found guilty of holding undisclosed property;
-National, German and Italian flags made by Jewish merchants and real-estate owners on order, and displayed on 10th May 1941; these were confiscated by police officers who roamed the streets of Bucharest on lorries to reclaim them.[29]

VI. Seizures and Requisitions

From the moment the Iron Guard came to power, they seized without payment:

29   It is said that these flags were preserved, and towns in occupied Bessarabia and Bucovina were decorated with them.

-almost all the Jewish schools in the country;
-almost all the Jewish hospitals in the country;
-most of the old people's homes and orphanages;
-several synagogues (these were converted into store houses,
gymnasiums, etc.);
-automobiles owned by Jews.

VII. Expulsions

While the Iron Guard were carrying out robberies and violent acts, the authorities and certain private individuals hunted Jews out of a large number of areas in the country—mostly Oltenia and Wallachia. This situation, created by the Iron Guard, remained the same even after their fall. In places where the violence of the Iron Guard manifested itself on a greater level (Targoviste, Giurgiu, Turnu Magurele, Caracal) not even 20% of the Jewish population, as of 6th September 1940, survived. Jews were also chased out of Panciu at the time of the earthquake on 10th November 1940.

During the reign of the Iron Guard, members of the Gendarmerie also banished Jews, especially from villages in the counties of Bihor and Suceava.

VIII. Evacuations

For two weeks following the outbreak of the war, Jews were evacuated from villages and almost every country town by order of the Leader of the State.[30] More than forty thousand people were made homeless. Almost half of them were transported several hundred kilometers away—under horrible conditions— where they existed in misery for more than two months. Their situation did not improve during the war years, only a very small number of them were allowed to return to their town of origin.

30   General Order of the Ministry of the Interior No.4147 on June 21,
      1941, signed by I. Popescu, Deputy Secretary of State.

IX. Internment and Hostages

During the reign of the Iron Guard Jews were already being sent individually to the concentration camp at Targu Jiu. Internment continued on a much larger scale following the outbreak of war. Entire populations were interned in certain areas (Constan, Siret, Darabani), in others (Galati, Ploiesti, Husi, Dorohoi) every healthy man, and in more (Piatra Neamt, Focsani, Felticeni, Buzau) most men were interned.[31]

X. Ghettos

At the beginning of August, following the occupation of Bessarabia and Bucovina, the survivors in these regions were collected from he Jewish communities, and placed in five centers. Their numbers on 1st September 1941 were the following[32]:

-in the ghettos of Secureni and Edine (Hotin county):   20,909;
-in the Marculesti ghetto (Soroca county):   10,737
-in the Vertujeni ghetto (Soroca county):   24,000
-in the town of Chernovitz: 49,497[33]

XI. Deportations

Between September 1941 and October 1942 one third of the surviving Jewish population of the country was deported beyond the Dnyester. The property of deportees was either confiscated, robbed or destroyed. The circumstances in which the deportation took place led to the death of large numbers en route. Half of those who arrived at the concentration camps and ghettos of Transnistna perished during the first winter. The survivors lived in the most miserable conditions imaginable; they were surrounded by illness, hunger and other hardships; they suffered the terror of never ending harassment, and feared death every moment.

31   General Order of the Ministry of the Interior No.4599 on June 30, 1941.

XII. Withdrawal of the Right to Work

Even before the Iron Guard system, the creation of a legal status for Jews, ensured their exclusion from most possible posts.

(a) In The Field of Freelance Work

32   On September 1, 1941 the populations of Bessarabia and Bucovina were counted. These figures date back to these counts but have never been officially confirmed. However, they definitely reflect reality and this can easily be proved if we compare them with figures shown in contemporary official decrees and reports:

According to report No.7151 of September 1, 1941, from the Gendarmerie Head Office in Chernovitz, addressed to the Highest Military Tribunal, the number of Jews in concentration camps in Hotin county was as follows:

The count:	Compiled by Gendarmes:	Estimated by local authorities:
Edineti Camp	12,248	11,224
Secureni Camp	10,201	8,302
Total:	22,449	19,526

According to report No.1140 on August 30, 1941 of the Bessarabian Gendarmerie Head Office addressed to the Highest Military Tribunal, at this time there were 22,969 Jews in Vertujeni Camp.

In the report of General Ion Topor, the Chief Military Judge of the army, compiled under order No.5023 B. on September 4, 1941 from General Headquarters, there is also the figure 22,969 regarding the camp at Vertujeni. However, also according to this report, there were 10,356 Jews in Secureni, in Edineti 11,762 and in Kishinev, 10,400, who were locked up in camps. The deporta-

The right to practice was withdrawn—with few exceptions—from Jewish lawyers, engineers, architects, journalists, consultants and pharmacists. The law regulating the practice of medicine strictly limited the field of practice for Jewish doctors.

(b) In: State-run and Private Companies

With the application of the Iron Guard law ordering the Romanianization of company employees, strong actions were taken to ensure the dismissal of Jewish officials from private companies.[34]

All Jewish public officials had already been dismissed as a result of their new legal status.

> tion to Transnistria was ordered on the basis of this report. However, in instructions issued by the Gendarmerie Office of Kisinev (Colonel T. Meculescu), only 22,150 Jews were mentioned in relation to the deportation to the camp of Vertujeni

33   The Jews of Chernovitz were ghettoized on October 11, 1941 by order of Directive No.37 from General Corneliu Calotescu, Governor of Bucovina, issued on October 10.

34   In one report by Dr. C. Danulescu, Minister of labor, dated March 1943, regarding the dismissal of Jewish employees from their places of work, the situation is the following:

On August 1, 1941, 28,225 Jews were employed by 8,126 firms;

On December 13, 1941, 16,292 Jews were employed by 7,647 firms;

On March 1, 1943, 6,506 Jews were employed by 4,301 firms.

Antonescu wrote the following resolution in this report:

"Very good. The operation should be continued. However difficult this might be under present circumstances, we have to achieve total Romanianization We will have to complete this by the time the war ends. The Ministry of labor must do everything possible to find the most effective method of achieving this aim. It will be given a free hand on this issue."

(c) Craftsmen

The certificates of trade, work-books, and contracts of Jewish apprentice craftsmen were invalidated by the Ministry of labor with unduly Draconian—and in a large number of cases unlawful - directives.

Although some craftsmen were able to safeguard their right to work through concessions, such arrangements were illusory, since the apprentices in question had to spend almost all of their time in labor service anyway.

(d) In the Fields of Commerce and Industry

The sphere of economic activities involving Jews, which had been severely reduced as a consequence of their new legal status, was diminished further as a result of a series of decrees. They were expelled from the boards of public limited companies; barred from commercial activities in villages; prevented from merchandising alcoholic drinks; prohibited from selling official forms in the Romanian language; from trading in leather, iron, grain; from working in the tourist and travel industry, and film industry, etc. With the help of the law on company registration, it became possible to refuse registration to all Jewish firms. The most was made of this opportunity. /.../

XIII. Labor Service

The autumn of 1940 witnessed the beginning of Jews used as "labor for public use" under the orders of county heads and mayors (later a separate decree referred to this as "obligatory labor"). It became a legal obligation in December 1940, and was organized under the supervision of the army from 1st August, 1941.[35] For the following three years, almost without respite (the only considerable break took place in the winter of 1941/42) more than 150,000 Jews—men and women—were forced to carry out difficult, and often completely exhausting work on roads, railway lines and quarries. They had to sweep streets, clear snow, remove the dead and wounded from debris following bomb attacks, defuse unexploded devices, etc. Although the law imposed obligatory work only for those between the ages of 18 and 50, administrative abuses extended the age limit in both directions, and children of sixteen and old people over seventy were also among those forced into labor. /... / Jews driven into labor service found themselves constantly under the threat of severe punishment, ranging from corporal punishment to deportation—to Transnistria—of family members, and death.[36]

XIV. Forced Financial Contributions

The Jews, who had been deprived of the right to work, and impoverished as a result of the above-mentioned litany of burdens and suffering, were

35   The first directive in relation to this is by Ion Antonescu. It was formulated and signed by General I. Popescu (Jack), Deputy Secretary of State of the Ministry of the Interior - who died before atoning for his sins-; the text of Directive No.5811 of July 18, 1941 is the following:

"General Antonescu, the Leader of the State, has formally ordered that Jews in labor camps or military prison camps should be used for physical labor.

If anyone escapes, every tenth person must be shot dead.

If they do not work as they should, no food shall be given to them, and neither should they be allowed to receive or buy food.

Measures are to be taken to ensure the execution of this directive.

Brigadier-General Ion Popescu m.p.,

Deputy State Secretary, Rank of Minister"

36   General Directives No.55500 of June 27, 1942 from the Chiefs of Staff, who regulated the labor service of Jews, ordered the following forms of punishment under point D.8:

"f/ to punish minor misdemeanors committed within the framework of labor force troops (arriving late for assembly, undisciplined behavior, etc.) the commander will use corporal punishment based on the regulations of military service.

also forced to bear financial sacrifices, some of which have already been enumerated in the first section of this chapter.

XV. Miscellaneous

Throughout the four-year period, a complete series of directives was introduced, through both legal and administrative means. These competed with one another to increase the oppression and misery of Jews, and contributed further to their impoverishment.

The Iron Guard organized the boycott of Jewish enterprises, signs saying "Jewish shop" were put on them, and armed Iron Guard members blocked the entrances to shops to prevent people from going inside.

The Iron Guard government barred all Jewish students from state schools and universities.

g/ Jews will be sent to Transnistria with their families (father, mother, wife, children) for physical labor, or to ghettos if they commit the following crimes:

- Repeated minor misdemeanors mentioned in paragraph

-   If they do not work conscientiously, or avoid work through means of fraud, bribes, the abuse of personal contacts; if they fail to present themselves after being called up for labor service; if they stop working without permission, or if they abstain from work, etc.;

-   If they do not inform the Recruiting Center of their change of address, regardless of whether they change address within the same town or move from one town to another, even if the Ministry of the Interior gives them permission to do so;

-   If they establish sexual relationships with Romanian women;

-   If male criminals do not present themselves voluntarily, or cannot be located by the police, their families will be sent to Transnistria."

It was forbidden for Jews to own radios; to employ Christian servants; shop at markets at certain hours; to walk in the streets of various towns at certain times of day; to go to swimming pools or baths; to frequent certain restaurants; to travel from one town to another; to buy directly from peasants, etc.

In some towns Jews had to wear signs to distinguish them from other residents. This was the source of many serious incidents, paralyzing the activities of those who might still have had a chance. [37]

The food stamps of Jews were marked to be valid for decreased portions, often twenty per cent of their original value. For certain foodstuffs, especially flour and corn products, Jews were not provided with any rations at all. For a long time Jews had to pay twice as much for bread as the rest of the population.

Those Jews living on expropriated Jewish property had to pay a higher rent at first than the other tenants; later they were legally barred from extending their tenure, and forcibly evicted without exception; including former owners, against whom expropriation laws had not been introduced. Jews living on the property of Christian owners were generally barred from extending their tenure until April 1943, and it was left to them to choose between an arbitrarily increased rent or eviction.

Centuries-old Jewish cemeteries (in Bucharest, Iasi, Buzau, Moineti, Siret, etc.) were destroyed, bones removed, and gravestones either discarded or used to pave roads and yards.

37   The obligation to wear the distinguishing sign was extended to the whole country by Directive number 8368 on September 2,1941 by the Ministry of the Interior, but was withdrawn on September 8 following the energetic protest of the President of the Union of Jewish Religious Communities.

Those Responsible for the Atrocities

The responsibility for the cruel and terrible acts against the Jewish population lies with the Romanian government, and personally with Ion Antonescu and his two governments, as well as part of the Romanian nation, especially the small-town petit bourgeoisie, which included the administrative apparatus, the army, the press, the judicial establishment, the clergy, teachers, guilds, free-lancers, and members of the business community.

The dictator and his ministers are guilty and accountable, because:

1. With their relentless propaganda and manipulated press they contributed to the formation of an atmosphere which provided unlimited opportunities for bloodbaths and looting.

2. Their unholy decrees and administration tolerated and supported robberies, murders and other lawless activities committed by the Iron Guard regime.

3. Through their introduction of a law providing for the expropriation of property, they organized the theft of Jewish property.

4. They ordered the eviction of the Jewish population from villages and towns, thus forcing Jews towards the path of hopeless flight and annihilation.

5. They tolerated and encouraged the atrocities committed by invading armies, which resulted in the slaughter of 150,000 Jews.

6. With a devious communique they hypocritically instigated the bloodbath in Iasi on 29 and 30 June 1941.

7. They ordered the deportations in Bessarabia and Bucovina, during which two thirds of the Jewish population, who had survived the bloodbaths of these regions, perished. Aiding deportees was prohibited for a long time, and won the approval of the authorities only when the epidemics,

which had begun to rage in the camps, threatened to endanger the rest of the population.

8. The seizure of deportees' property was at first tolerated and later legalized.

9. Bloody retaliation was ordered and executed. Following an explosion in Odessa, which was claimed to have been sabotage, more than 20,000 innocent people, the majority of whom were Jewish, were killed.

10. Labor service was legally introduced and ordered. In the course of three years more than 150,000 people (men, women, children and the elderly) were forcibly dragged away for the purposes of compulsory slave labor.

11. Obligatory fees and contributions of considerable amounts were legally imposed on impoverished Jews to squeeze even more money out of them.

12. Almost the entire Jewish population was deprived of one of the basic human rights: the right to work.

13. Jewish students were barred from all the universities in the country; driven out of every state school and Christian private school; and an attempt was made to abolish Jewish schools altogether.

14. The spirit and practice of Hitler's laws were introduced into Romanian legislation.

15. The traditional elders of Jewish religious communities were removed and replaced by a police organization modeled on the German system introduced in occupied Europe. Its aim was to cleanse Romania of Jews.

16. The death penalty was introduced for certain crimes if they were committed by Jews; this applied to children as young as fifteen. [1]

17. For four years Jews lived in an atmosphere of panic and terror, which mentally and physically eroded those who had managed to survive the bloodbaths.

18. The administrative apparatus of the country, with its traditional desire to persecute the weak, especially Jews, obediently executed the anti-Semitic commands and decrees of guilty state legislators. It often stepped outside the framework of these directives, or even acted against central orders so as to increase the intensity of this persecution by acting on its own initiative.

Among the most guilty members of the administrative apparatus were the governors of occupied territories (Bessarabia, Bucovina and Transnistria)

1   Law No 698 published on September 2, 1942 in edition No.221 of the Official Gazette, ordered the death penalty for all Jews—male or female—over the age 15 who returned to the country illegally after being deported to Transnistria.

Dictator Antonescu wrote the following into report No.36945 on May 10, 1944 by the Gendarmerie Office regarding the Jews who crossed the border to escape the hell in Hungary:

"The public must be notified.

Jews illegally crossing the border must be shot dead, as must those who offer them refuge or fail to report them. Action must be taken within 24 hours.

I asked Ambassador Mr Killinger to send German guards to border crossings. These guards—along with our guards—will check all those who wish to cross.

If someone cannot identify himself, force should be employed to find out his identity.

The entire length of the frontier must be guarded strictly.

Raids must be held periodically throughout the whole country."

The Military Cabinet of the Leader of the State ordered the Ministry of the Interior to execute these orders through Directive number 205396 of May 16, 1944.

The law ordering the death penalty appeared under number 301 in edition number 123 of the Official Gazette on May 29, 1944.

Of the three governors of Bucovina, only General Corneliu Calotescu can be held accountable. Similarly, of the governors of Transnistria, only the first, G. Alexianu, a teacher, is guilty and can be held responsible, and county heads working as their subordinates; /.../ The governors were guilty of and responsible for the organization and execution of deportations as well as the misery, terror and starvation to which deportees were subjected. Members of the first—Iron Guard—group of county heads were rivals in creating and sustaining an atmosphere of panic and terror, and contenders in the violent robbery of Jews. The members of the second group, almost without exception, were officers who diligently, and frequently with extreme zeal, executed the series of shocking measures introduced at the outbreak of war: evacuations from villages and towns; the arrest and internment of hostages; the compulsory display of distinguishing signs; the organization of the first labor service squads; curfews; the restriction of shopping time at markets; restriction of movement, and the confinement of Jews to certain districts. Mayors and police chiefs played major roles in the persecution of Jews.

The army had always been the bastion of anti-Semitism. Romanian pseudo-democracy must be held accountable for supporting and spreading the hatred, with which the national elite regarded Jewish citizens and democratic, progressive tendencies.

Both the Iron Guard movement and the war itself helped strengthen this violently and barbarically manifested hatred, with its terrible consequences. A pretext was advanced that Jews supposedly insulted and offended the army during its withdrawal from territories given-up in 1940. The Romanian army, upon re-occupation of these territories in the same year, wreaked foul revenge; with savage anger, over a period of weeks, more than 150,000 Jews—men, women, the elderly and children—were exterminated. With an insatiable thirst for blood, they launched attacks on innocent people. These were their military operations. An incredibly large amount represented itself in the band of uniformed criminals from the rank and file of the army, from chief commanders to privates.

The army played a detestable part in both the organization and supervision of Jewish slave labor, and the planning and direction of deportations in 1941; in the preparation and partial execution of the mass deportations in the autumn of 1942, and in the application of several anti-Semitic measures in areas close to the front (distinguishing signs, expulsions from villages, travel restrictions, etc.).

Even though members of the judiciary cannot be listed among those who would literally have been guilty of war crimes, and while some of them attempted to uphold the—fundamental principles of the law, when the persecution began, they showed a complete cessation of jurisdiction, and completely vanished from the scene at the time of the Iron Guard terror. However, they were tremendously alert and persistent - literally, and even more so—in the application of racist laws. Since the Iron Guard movement had a strong influence on it, primarily on the younger cadres, it played an important role in the development of this movement, especially with the fact that it guaranteed immunity for every unlawful act committed before 1940. Large numbers of judges—and officers—were the beneficiaries of racist laws; they were primarily involved in the expulsion of Jews from their homes so that they themselves could become the new occupants.

The press completely and unreservedly placed itself at the disposal of the fascist dictatorship. The system protected it by silencing, through bans and intimidation, all newspapers and journalists displaying opposition, objectivity, or even reservations concerning the activities of the government. The press, in its entirety; with remarkable zeal, undertook the unholy role of poisoning public opinion. Through its constant perpetuation of smear campaigns and hatred, it incited people to rob and murder. Its creation of such a gloomy atmosphere aided the criminal activities of the government. While cataloguing the organs and journalists involved would be pointless, it would not be an overstatement, however, to accuse the press, between 1940 and 1944, of being the most important agent—a genuine fifth column of Romanian Nazi and anti-Semitic propaganda.

Priests and teachers played an important role in poisoning the minds of the masses. From their pulpits and desks they propagated the hatred which later led to bloody massacres and horrifying robberies. Many priests and teachers personally took part in and were the beneficiaries of acts of robbery and murder.

Societies and guilds, with few exceptions, along with free-lance workers, displayed their disgusting opportunism; they profited enormously from the boom created by political prosperity.

Directly following the fascist dictatorship's seizure of power in Romania, almost all public and private bodies which represented any community in whatever capacity, professional, scientific, cultural, or other, attempted in earnest, beginning with the swift expulsion of Jews, to prove their ability to adapt to the new regime. Their number is an indication of how the Romanian intelligentsia behaved on an institutional level.

The only professional body which still endorsed the activities of its Jewish members was the Board of Physicians. However, Jewish doctors were later ghettoized following their expulsion from the medical community. Medical practice was also strictly organized along racist ethnic lines; Jewish doctors were forbidden to treat Christian patients and vice versa.

The merchant class, a major beneficiary of the anti-Semitic regime and new boom, was at the forefront of the early stages of the persecution.

The Iron Guard plunder was always shared in a brotherly fashion between merchants (the instigators hiding behind the scenes) and the bandits who committed the crimes. The first economic measures taken against Jews—always justified as the necessary safeguarding of Romanian interests—were always debated and decided in the witches' den of Romanian merchants. Following each new measure which excluded a certain group of Jewish merchants from commercial life or facilitated the continuation of their activities, benefactors appeared offering to protect the Jewish firms with their Aryan shields. The majority of these benefactors, who prospered at the expense of Jews, behaved despicably when the subject of returning some of the goods entrusted to them arose.

This was what the terror and persecution wreaked against Jews looked like in Romania. It had its beginnings in the lunatic instincts of the enemies of mankind. It was initiated and ordered by the criminal leaders of the state, executed and supported by a section of the Romanian nation. Even though this section of society was not the majority, if we take into consideration their mentality and the times they lived in, it was the most typical.

The Iron Guard Government

September 6, 1940 - January 21, 1941

General Ion Antonescu was promoted from virtual anonymity. On September 5, 1940 he was summoned before the Presidium of the Council of Ministers. On the following day he was bestowed with dictatorial powers, and entrusted with governing the country.

Regaining consciousness from the dreadful shock caused by the dizzying train of the events, Romanian public opinion was confused and at a loss when it came to receiving this unknown saviour.

Only very few had paid attention to his ephemeral and trace less roles in previous reactionary governments. Even fewer were aware of his activities in senior military institutions. He was said to be an energetic soldier who did not tolerate opposition, but also indecisive and easily influenced; there were whispers that he was vain, haughty, and that he loved both praise and servile fawning; everybody knew that he was wicked, quick-tempered and predisposed to violence. Throughout his entire career he was taunted with the name "Red Dog". The country, unhinged by the sequence of recent happenings, dazed by the political chaos, and hypnotized by the clever manipulation of the general atmosphere, received him with doubt tempered with traditional indifference and skepticism. A certain section of the population sensed the unavoidable menace from the very outset. Hannibal had noisily and violently announced his arrival at the doors of Israel's tents.

The omens of the ensuing storm had appeared two months before. The pogrom in Dorohoi and the spread of its lesser effects to the towns and villages of South Bucovina; the murder of Jews thrown out of moving trains; the incitement to hatred and murder by the press; in the way state legislators Horia Sima and Radu Budisteanu were gnashing their teeth, and finally in the shameful anti-Semitic directives issued by I. V. Gruia, Minister of Justice, along with his vile reasoning. Collectively these facts represented the tornado that had entrapped the tormented Jews, and forced them to notice the thick black clouds towering over their heads; clouds which were to cover that sky for four years.

Days went by, and events unfolded. General Antonescu became the head of government, a leader of state endued with dictatorial power; the members of the Iron Guard, who were increasingly becoming the rulers of the streets, were marching, organizing patrols and singing - for the meanwhile only singing - their songs of hatred, blood and death, and the sky had not yet burst, and the earth had not yet opened to swallow the Jews awaiting their "inevitable fate".

There were only one or two incidents, a little over-zealousness, or as the General said "some romance and fervor".

The scattered beatings of Jews on the streets, the looting of some richer Jews, and attempts at organizing an economic boycott urged Horia Sima to write a circular to Iron Guard groups, in which he admits—after hardly more than five days in government (on September 11, 1940)—that there have been insignificant incidents in the country as a consequence of the change in system".

The Jewish political leadership made its presence felt from the start, and the President of the Union of Jewish Communities turned directly to General Antonescu. At a meeting on September 14, Dr. W. Filderman lists the abuses and unlawful actions—committed either by petty thieves or ministers—which had piled up during only eight days of the new government. At this first meeting of the two leaders (between whom, from this time forth, there was to be a long, ruthless but unequal battle) the General is both kind and brimming with goodwill. He is surprised by what he hears, and promises to make amends for everything. He orders the removal of certain "Jewish shop" signs, instructs the Minister of Education to reverse the decision to abolish the Jewish religion, and shouts at the Minister of the Interior, on the phone: "Petrivicescu! Your "guys" are misbehaving, and bringing shame on me!". Finally, he asks for the support of Jews, asks them not to wind up their businesses, and says that they should pursue their own trades, and thus provides hope that situation will not worsen or a tragic event will not occur. He even backs up his promises in writing, and two days later the Office of the Leader sends a transcript from the Presidium of the Council of Ministers to the Union of Jewish Communities containing the following extract:

"I ensure Mr. Filderman that if his co-religionists do not openly or secretly sabotage the political or economic life of the system, then no harm will be done to Jewish citizens. The words of General Antonescu are not to be taken lightly."

Even though "the words of General Antonescu are not to be taken lightly", abuses are growing nearby in the capital; beatings on the streets are multiplying; the houses of Jews are being searched, and winter food reserves are especially singled out for robbery; the automobiles of Jews are forcibly removed from garages and streets. As a result, the Minister of the Interior feels it necessary to make an announcement which does not attempt to hide the shameful situation:

"We would like to draw everybody's attention to the fact that recent abuses have been committed by forces alien to the Iron Guard movement so as to discredit the government's actions, which had been taken to ensure the reestablishment of order."

The "guys" acted more conscientiously in the villages than in the capital. In Buzau the Iron Guard police arrested at least twenty young Zionists between the ages of 16 and 20. After torturing them into confessing to being communists, all of them were sent to the Military Tribunal. They were obviously acquitted, but later had to pay a terrible price for the Iron Guard's joke. They remained "stigmatized" in the files of the State Security Service and were later deported to Transnistria where almost all of them were killed.

In Arad about 40 Jews, selected from the leaders of the community, were arrested without reason, tortured, beaten, and kept in the police station for several days.

In Calarasi Urziceni, Buzau, Ramnicul Sarat, Roman and elsewhere "Jewish shop" was scrawled on the shop windows and trade-signs of Jewish shops, and there were calls for a boycott. Furthermore, in Buzau Iron Guard patrols threateningly prevented people from entering Jewish shops. A synagogue was also attacked by a band of Iron Guards in the same place, during the first days. Praying people were searched, robbed and arrested for a night.

In Iasi, the birthplace of the Cuza hooligans, and later that of the Codreanu Iron Guards, the barbaric terror started in the first days. Hundreds of Jews were dragged into police cellars or Iron Guard "nests", where they were beaten, tortured and robbed. Later it turned out that this act of terror had been organized to extort money from the Jews. After they had come to an agreement with the leaders of the Iron Guard organization to pay them 6,000,000 lei, the violence against them ceased for a long time.

During the first days a few of the "guys," who later became ministers, were even more diligent than the petty thieves.

Radu Budisteanu, the Minister of Education, who felt how unstable the velvet chair under him was, through the famous directives of September 11, 1940, attempted to write himself into the annals of history by removing the Jewish religion from among the list of acknowledged religions thus making its practice impossible.

The same minister, who became the executioner of Jewish schools before 6 September, with his directive on August 31, 1940, was anxious to chase Jewish actors out of all national and private theatres—before his resignation—and to forbid the purchase of religious relics from Jewish dealers. He resigned from politics on September 14, 1940 after a long talk with the Leader of the Union of Jewish Communities, Dr. W. Filderman and the chief-rabbi, Dr. Al. Safran; this time he invalidated his own directives, and suspended the measures he took against the Jewish religion. The following day he was no longer a minister.

His successor as Minister of Education, Professor Traian Braileanu surpassed his predecessor. He created a type of Jewish ghetto of artists with a prescribed repertoire, and obliged them to call themselves "Jewish Theater". He organized the boycott of Jewish book-shops by prohibiting officials, the staffs of schools and even school children from shopping there. He, however, also found it advisable to invalidate measures aiming the annihilation of the Jewish religion.

The Minister of Justice, I. V. Gruia, whose shirt was not as green as those of his colleagues, won gold stars for his preparation of the famous 'regulations for Jews'. But, he will be really successful only later, when he defends Jews—as their well-paid lawyer—in the course of legal actions taken against them based on laws prepared by him. At present he is busy chasing Jewish judges, bailiffs and public prosecutors from their posts, and forbidding Jewish lawyers—with the help of a special law—from holding executive positions in the Law Society and from practicing their profession at military tribunals.

During the first month of the existence of the National Iron Guard State, professional bodies, especially those of the intelligentsia, were very hard-working. Their list of activities is long, shamefully so. However, it is our duty to mention it.

Heading the list is the First Incorporated Law Society of the country. On September 6, 1940, simultaneously with the start of the new system, the Incorporated Law Society of the capital also secured its own day of historical importance by removing the first group of Jewish lawyers, who had identified themselves as Jews in compliance with the directives against Jews. Fifty-five lawyers were expelled on that day, only because the counselors soon tired of the task.

During the following days they compensated for the backlog caused by the their weariness on the first day; through rushed, superficial and dictatorial decisions arrived at during six meetings (on September 6, 7, 10, 11, 12 and 13) out of the 1,479 Jewish lawyers only 177 escaped with the right to practice their profession.

One week later the Incorporated Law Society was followed by the Society of Romanian Engineers, which expelled the first group of Jewish engineers from its membership on September 3, and went to great lengths to emphasize: it had no intention of abiding by any directive which would have enabled certain people to maintain their rights, and saw to it that the second and last group of Jewish engineers were also expelled. During the next meeting (on October 10), the Society's "cleansing of Jews" was completed.

Then the flood gates opened. On September 20 the Sports Association invalidated the identity cards of Jewish journalists; on September 21 the Department of Social Security dismissed Jewish deliverers, and on the same day the Romanian Opera dismissed its Jewish employees. On September 25 the Trade Union of Journalists excluded its Jewish members, on 25 the

Union of Professional Journalists rid itself of Jews, on 29 the Council of the Association of the Chambers of Commerce "homogenized its leadership with the help of Romanian elements".

At the beginning of October and November those embarrassed about lagging behind were anxious to close the gap. On October 4 the Union of Romanian Writers, on 6th the Trade Union of Journalists of Bucovina, on 7th the Society of the Licensed Electricians, on 10th the National Union of Dentists, and on the same day the Society of Entrepreneurs for Public Works, on the following day the Society of Architects (on the occasion of their 50th anniversary), followed by the Trade Union of Artists (October 12), the Romanian Society of Eye, Ear and Throat Specialists (October 12) the National Society of Chemical Engineers (October 17), the "Scenic Romania" Board of Tourism (October 26), the Campina Chamber of Commerce, the Society of Endocrinologists (October 30), the Society of Bucharest Abattoir Butchers (October 30), the Society of Romanian Publicists (November 8), the Directorship of Boxers, Wrestlers, etc. (November 8), and last but not least, on November 10, the National Society of University Professors and the Society of Deaf and Dumb People expelled their Jewish colleagues and members.

September ended with a sensational interview, given by General Antonescu to the Italian newspaper *"Stampa"*; this was made public by the Bucharest newspapers on September 30, together with detailed explanations and praise for the "leader" as well as insults and outbursts of hatred aimed at Jews.

This was the first time the general publicly and substantially dealt with the Jewish issue; this was the first time he started to make threats: changes, dismissals, expropriation, expatriation—this was what the Leader mentioned in his first announcement regarding the fate of a population of 400,000, which had set root in the country centuries previously, and played such an important role in its development, a role which could not be compared to that played by all the other minorities put together.

The general said the following, word for word:

"The economy and capital of Romania is in the hands of the Jews. They also had a monopoly on credit. Real Romanians have been sidelined by these aliens because the governments of Romania have not provided them with credit and access to the economic market. However, companies directed by Romanians also exist in Romania, and these prove the excellent ability of our race".

"I will solve the Jewish issue in the course of reorganizing the state. I will gradually substitute Jews with Romanians, first of all with members of the Iron Guard, who will prepare themselves for this in the meantime. We will expropriate the greatest part of Jewish property, and will compensate them for this. Jews who entered the country after 1913, in other words after the second Balkan War, will be expatriated as soon as possible, regardless of whether they become Romanian citizens in the interim. While this is taking place, we will substitute the others, as I have already said, step by step. Jews will have be allowed to live in this country, but will not have the opportunity to be the beneficiaries of its resources and wealth. Firstly, it must be the Romanians who live in Romania, they must assume worthier positions; the others can only come after them, if there are free places left."

If the first month of Iron Guard rule was the period of experimentation and randomly testing the water, the second was designed to lay sound foundations and organize everything in the fur their interest of the German Empire and Iron Guard movement.

During this period members of the Iron Guard penetrated into the deepest corners of the state and all sectors of the economy; this was the time of the dubious and unprepared elements which flooded all the large commercial and industrial companies as commissars of Romanianization; this was the time when the Minister of the Interior and the managing director of the State Security Organization, the trustees of peace and order, replaced the professional policemen of central and other police stations throughout the whole country with absolutely unprepared people (graduates from Arts Faculties, Business Colleges and schools, etc.). It was known that these would barbarically engage in acts of terror without any inhibitions and oblige in a way similar to the Iron Guard uprising already on the horizon; this was the time of the preparation and enactment of those foul bills which would later become the basis for acts of looting and persecution.

On the basis of a prepared plan, into which the general atmosphere was calculated (the atmosphere which forced a constant climate of tension and panic on its victims), the racist laws of the Iron Guard system followed in quick succession in an endless flow of suffering. The racist legislation of the Iron Guard was not constructed on any basic tenets of law or justice; it lacked morality and logic and even its guiding ideology—be it nationalist or ultra-nationalist—was simply the shameful weapon employed by the state and its leaders to rob unprotected victims, just as lowly bandits used clubs and pistols.

The justification for these laws, which served as models for many clerks for four years, will remain as monuments to judicial stupidity, the misrepresentation of the truth and the cynical mockery of morality and benevolence.

The Iron Guard did not maintain the dizzying speed at which it introduced racist legislation, and neither did such legislation encompass all sectors at first under threat. The reasons for this lie neither in the benevolent hesitation of the Iron Guard leadership nor in any peculiar resistance by state governors. The Iron Guard's passion for fighting and looting did not let up for a moment, between September 6, 1940 and January 21,1941. In part, however, they achieved weak results through their recourse to the law since the spoils had to be shared with the state, which received the lion's share. Furthermore, terror used parallel with legislation proved much more effective because it excluded competition from the state, thus securing for individuals themselves all that they had yearned for, or items to which they had laid personal claims. This can serve to explain the suspension of Iron Guard racist legislative activity in the middle of November, by which stage the terror had started to blossom and it was becoming increasingly clear why the Iron Guards were not expropriating Jewish real estate in towns or that belonging to commercial and industrial firms.

The shameful Iron Guard legislature started to work on October 3, 1940 by issuing a legally enforceable decree. /... /

Bills providing for serious, organized and meticulous robbery were passed two days later. On the holiday of October 6, which the Iron Guards organized for themselves to celebrate their first month in control of the country, General Antonescu honored the "guys" with many gifts.

The Captain of the Metropolitan Police, General Dona, was replaced by a member of the Iron Guard Senate, Colonel Stefan Zavoianu, whose criminal disposition could be used to extend the acts of terror (he appeared in a green shirt at the Iron Guard celebration); Zavoianu also announced the law concerning the appointment of the officer in charge of Romanianization and the expropriation of rural Jewish property.

The simultaneous appearance of these two laws signaling the beginning of robberies and looting, is characteristic and significant.

The law of October 14, which organized the ghettoization of schools, was introduced soon after the announcement of these basic laws. /.../

Two very important laws succeeded each other: one affecting doctors on November 15, and the other affecting company employees on November 16.

Every set of statistics indicates, and all avenues of research agree on the fact that one of the basic problems in Romanian society was the lack of physicians, and the consequences of this were catastrophic for the Romanian nation. The worrying spread of the so-called national diseases, and the infant mortality rate which was much higher than the average figures in other nations—these two facts were eloquently pointed out with an enormous amount evidence by all those who dealt with the basic issue of the health of the Romanian nation. The solution recommended was always the same—irrespective of how much the political and social views of the researchers varied—that the number of town and village doctors had to be increased, and more emphasis should be placed on health care.

In spite of this, there was a government, the Iron Guard government, which not only did nothing towards providing a remedy for the much warned endemic, but with a simple directive—aimed at satisfying the savage impulses of certain members—expelled a great number of doctors from the Board of Physicians, thus catastrophically diminishing the originally small number entrusted with caring for the health of a nation.

With the law of November 15, 1940, under the threat of severe penalties, Jewish doctors were prohibited from treating non-Jewish patients. In order to avoid misunderstandings, Jewish doctors were forced to clearly indicate on all their prescription slips and advertisements that they were "Jewish doctors", irrespective of whether they had been university professors, or lecturers.

The other law enacted on November 16, 1940, which was named after its creator, Iascinski, /... / proved to be much more inhumane.

This law obliged all forms of public and private companies to dismiss all their Jewish employees within a given period of time, not later than 31 December, 1941, "regardless of the method of payment, the time spent in employment, and conditions of office, including all apprentices, trainees and those who worked for the owner without pay."

Obviously, the legislators, were not influenced by any human considerations. Such an attitude could only be expected from those who gave their unrepentant support to the doctrine and practices of the Iron Guard: in most cases no compensation was paid by the owners to those dismissed. Even though the national economy was seriously destabilized by the demolition of its structural order, not even the slightest worry concerning this could be detected in the new law. The application of the law meant the replacement—over a short period of time—of one social stratum, united by the experience of many years, with elements who, in most cases, were completely ill-prepared, even if any sign of good-will could be detected in them at all.

The last shameful Iron Guard law, which appeared exactly on the day the revolt erupted, transformed the Jews' obligation to serve in the army into a compulsory financial and labor service.

What had previously been an patriotic obligation, now turned into a financial one. The legislature forced progressive taxes on Jews between the ages 18 and 50 based on a rate by which a young man who had not reached the age 24, paid tax not only consistent with his own income (if he had any) but also based on that of his parents, or his wife (and all taxable income of the spouse was to be included in the calculation). Consequently, a merchant to whom the unfortunate idea occurred of declaring an annual income of 1 million lei, was obliged to pay 249,235 lei in military tax as well as 415,392 in taxes and surtaxes.

Naturally, the activities of the Iron Guard legislature did not inhibit the endeavors of scoundrels, robbers, highway-men and barbarians, who created the atmosphere necessary for the massacres yet to come. In both the capital, and the remotest villages of the country, there were constant and unhindered acts of violence and looting, the aim of which was to weaken the resolve of Jews, both individually and as a community.

On October 31, following a discussion with the Chairmen of the Jewish Religious Communities, their leader, Dr. W. Filderman attended another meeting with General Antonescu. The general remarked, with his hypocritical kindness, well-known from the past, that he must surely be the only leader among the leaders of the Axis powers who maintains such a relationship with a Jewish leader. After this the conversation continued basically as follows:

"I'm aware of why you have come. I've heard that there has been some mistreatment but I've already taken measures to ensure that this won't happen again. I can see that you've brought an entire library with you again, but there's no need for so many files and complaints, because nothing like this will happen again."

"General, you asked me to tell Jews to continue their activities and not to tell anyone to stop. All of us listened to you but Iron Guards come and terrorize us with revolvers. In Cerna-Voda, for example, the authorities themselves forced certain local Jews to hand over their companies, which were worth of millions, for tens of thousands of lei. Those who objected were beaten up and tortured. Women's hair was cut off and then all of them were chased out of town."

"Mr. Filderman, it won't happen again."

"You gave an order to end the erection of Jewish shop signs. Your order was not obeyed, on the contrary, the boycott is spreading, and this is affecting the economy of the entire nation, not just Jews. These signs have also been stuck up in Calarasi, Buzau, Turnu Magurele, Urziceni and Orastie. In Ramnicul Valcea Iron Guard groups stand in front of Jewish shops all the time, and they won't let anybody enter. This was reported to the county head, who answered, 'There's nothing else to be done, close your shops.'."

"Don't worry about it, Mr. Filderman, it won't happen again."

"Jews are no longer able to travel by train. Traveling from one town to the other has become a form of torture for them. I receive letters and telegrams from everywhere reporting looting and torture, and all this happens in under the eyes of the authorities."

"I know. These have been reported to me, but they won't happen again." "The day before yesterday Iron Guards with revolvers poured into a house in Bucharest, the headquarters of the Sephardic Jewish Community. The chief rabbi was chased out of his flat. The offices of the Community and the Music Conservatory were emptied, people were chased out of their flats, and others took their places without right or legal formalities."

"Mr. Filderman, it won't happen again."

"In the provinces lands are being expropriated, not just brutally and ironhandedly, but with much abuse, and sometimes there are shameless acts of looting. In Saveni whole herds of cattle were taken away from Jews who trade in livestock, but who never had any land. In Braila a committee appointed by the deputy county head seized hundreds of wagons of grain, even though that grain was the property of Jewish exporters who had never had land in the village. At this very moment legions of the Gendarmerie in the towns and villages are busy taking an inventory of Jewish property. In certain places, like Ceice, in Bihar county, and Balaceanca, in Suceava county, these goods have been confiscated and removed. In Campulung-Bucovina the Mayor's Office has redrawn the town border 300 meters away from its original location to bring other parts of the towns within its jurisdiction, as villages, allowing for the expropriation Jewish property."

"This is indeed abuse. We do want to carry out the expropriation law gradually. But believe me, such abuses will cease."

"Also, in the name the expropriation law, the authorities have committed further abuses. Cemeteries, which are obviously on the outskirts of the town, have been deliberately expropriated so that they can be listed as council property. This has been the case in Ploesti, Buzau, Vaslui and even Bucharest. In Bacau, the town's agricultural engineer decided to sidestep the legal formalities of the expropriation law, and ordered the ploughing of the entire cemetery so that wheat could grow from the bones of Jews."

"He shouldn't have acted in that way. Look, I will order the return of the cemetery in Bucharest, and nothing like this will ever happen again."

"General, you are aware that because of laws and directives, our children have been chased out of state schools. Minister Braileanu scornfully remarked that he was not interested in the business of our education; we should organize this for ourselves. But our schools have been illegally confiscated and expropriated by force. Schools in Buceacea, Harlau, Vaslu and some in Bucharest have been taken from us.

"It won't happen again.

"General, in Orastie...

"It won't happen again. There won't be a repeat of this. No, no, no! I've already ordered /... /

Next day the terror started.

During the last three months of the Iron Guard government, Jewish citizens throughout the entire country lived in perpetual fear. During this time, in the territory of Romania there were almost 400,000 inhabitants to whom protection by state authorities was not extended. They not only lost their existential security and the protection of their property, moreover, they felt under threat in all places, and at all times. Those who were beaten or tortured had no means of defending themselves, to those who were looted and robbed all channels of complaint were closed. It was the same in every part of the country: if a Jew left home in the morning to go somewhere, it was not sure that he would return home in the evening. Those who stayed at home were startled by every noise, every knock on the door caused them to panic. In the villages and towns, in centrally located block of flats and poor huts, in the offices of bankers and factory owners, in the wooden hovels of pretzel vendors, and at the make-shift stalls of itinerant vendors, every Jew—regardless of how strong he was or how rich he was—lived in permanent agony from worrying about his own life and property or those of his neighbors.

Hundreds and thousands of Jews were tortured in the most horrible ways in the cellars of police stations and city halls, in the headquarters and nests of the Iron Guard, in their own flats or on the streets, on roads, meadows or in the depths of forests. Every murder and act of looting was committed with the support, initiation or direct supervision of organizations and persons whose duty in any normal, civilized state would be to protect the lives and property of its citizens.

Starting with the Minister of the Interior, General Constantin Petrovicescu, assisted by his Chef de Cabinet, Major Stelian Marinescu, but working independently of Lieutenant-Colonel Alexandru Riosianu; Alexandru Ghica, the Senior Director of the State Security Organization, aided by Director Maimuca and Police Inspector Baciu; three successive Chief Commissioners of the Metropolitan Police Force, General Dona, Colonel Stefan Zavoianu and Radu Mironovicic; every county head in Romania (all appointed under the directive of September 17, 1940)—a list modified only by one suicide and one dismissal for dishonesty, and finally almost every police superintendent in the country with outstanding contributions from the likes of Ilie Stanga (Bucharest), Paul Cojocaru (Ploiesti), Mazilu (Ploiesti), Hanu (Alba Julia), Ion Crisovan and Dr. Preda (Arad), Jura (Lugoj), Vespasian Lene (Sighisoara), Bucur Stavrescu (Targu Magurele), Vatasescu (Targoviste), Petre Zegheanu (Caracal), V. Stefanescu (Brasov), Radu Popian (Ramnicul Valcea), etc., all attempted to surpass one another in cruel beatings and uninhibited robberies.

Naturally, these people could not have committed so many acts of terror without a whole army of gangsters, and professional and amateur champions of the club, pistol and other means of torture. They were recruited from every class and section of the population; there were public officials among them (especially from ministries and county and town offices), private clerks, merchants, factory workers, lawyers, hooligans, engineers, robbers, doctors and tramps. All of them, irrespective of whether or not they were green-shirts, grandiloquently called themselves Iron Guards and committed their barbarically heroic deeds in the name of the "Iron Guard Movement". This was the only political representation of the country, and sanctioned as such by royal decree No.3151 on September 14, 1940.

From among the huge mass of lunatics, let us always remember the names of the following beasts: Mircea Petrovicescu, master of the torture center in the cellars of the Town Hall in the third "Albastru" district of Bucharest; Iron Guard Commander Stoia (Constanta); Ilie Colhon (Alba Julia); Grigoras Constantin, (Mayor of Targu Neamt), Dr. Silviu Craciunas (Piatra Neamt); Stefan Georgescu-Gorjan (Petrosani), engineer; Deputy Mayor Olteanu (Aiud); Dr. Stefan Milcoveanu, Dr. Popovici Lupa and Dr. Ruptureanu (Bucharest); Zozo Grigorescu (Ploiesti), lawyer; Mitica Dancila, Ion Dancila (Turda); Willy Janischewschi (Chairman of the Chamber of Commerce in Craiova); C. Pivniceru (Vaslui); Ion Bolfan (Mayor of Harlau village); Nicodem Borca (Deputy Mayor of the town of Deva); N. Craioveanu (Mayor of Lupeni); D. Ifrim (Chairman of the Chamber of Commerce in Bucharest); Professor Wertz (Arad), etc.

In this wilderness of hatred and brutality, not even one voice was raised in objection, not one whisper of hope could be heard. Naturally, I do not mean to suggest public statements or comments to the press. But, even at private gatherings, not one word of comfort was uttered for the sake of those had once been colleagues or friends.

It is also true that objections found their way onto the General's desk. In spite of being Romanian, there were those who claimed to have wrongly suffered in some way, and who, in spite of the wrongdoings they suffered, did not fail to lend their support to measures introduced against Jews. Voicu Nitescu, a minister during the era of pseudo- democracy, while complaining that his six-year-old son had been threatened with a revolver by members of the Iron Guard, took care to congratulate the General on the occasion of his birthday at the beginning of his complaint, and did not forget to emphasize that during his time at the Ministry of labor he went to great lengths to give labor an exclusively national character and to "remove from the field of labor those elements which constituted an obstacle to the complete nationalization of labor". In the following he denies his Jewish connections and points out, "I do not participate in any enterprise which functions with Semite capital, or which is run by Semites"......

One protest, however, should not be forgotten: it was delivered to General Antonescu by Mr. Iuliu Maniu, the former prime minister, on December 3, 1940, five days after the assassination of a number of politicians, including one of Mr. Maniu's close associates, Virgil Madgearu. Naturally, he was both hurt and enraged by these assassinations. However, the document also contained the following extract:

"On my part, General, I would like to ask you to reinforce the authority of the state without further delay; to entrust certain officials with ensuring order; to strive—through all means at your disposal—for a return to existential and financial security for all categories of citizens, since this alone can guarantee the continuity of productive work, which is so necessary for social and economic life.[2]

Iron Guard terror manifested itself in the most atrocious forms ever witnessed in the history of mankind. It began with arbitrary searches of houses, arrests, evictions, beatings, rape, torture; tying to shame-posts; individual and collective robberies, and culminated in the plundering and setting ablaze of churches, factories, shops and flats, and in the horrifying bloodbaths of the Iron Guard revolt.

This terror was organized by "the Iron Guard Movement" and by certain ministers led by the deputy prime minister, Horia Sima. However, the other members of the government encouraged them by tolerating their actions and providing them with immunity. The Leader of the State personally aided them through mindless legislation and administration.

The aims of Iron Guard terror varied according to the person or institution targeted. The country's Christian community was intimidated in order to paralyze the awakening of remorse in the few people whose united action could have led to the formation of a certain type of public opinion. Jews were to be eliminated from economic life; their property was to be robbed so that—irrespective of whether it was to become the possession of "members of the Iron Guard Movement"—an enormous weapon could be

2   In mentioning this statement made by the President of the National Party of Peasants, we must note the ambiguity and unclear formulation, which inevitably forces us to ask whether Mr Iliu Maniu included Jews in "all types of citizens"?

forged to assist the final aim: Iron Guard control of state administration and regulatory forces.

Naturally, power seized by Iron Guard members was at the expense of the Jews. The fight was very easy, and the rewards for both the Iron Guard and individuals were well worth the trouble. It seems that the signal for the outbreak of terror was given on November 1. Firstly, all kinds of thugs were allowed to operate freely, at most, they had to take into account local initiatives and instructions. This was how Iron Guard leaders tested the resistance of Jews and the possible reactions of the Leader of the State. The events of the first eight days, though characterized by violence, at times fatal, were nonetheless incoherent. In Turda a few Jews were tortured in order to acquire a long-envied distillery; in Caracal and Corabia a few shops were looted and the victims evicted; in Gaesti an attempt was made to violently acquire a few businesses; in Bucharest arrests became more and more widespread, beatings grew increasingly savage, etc. The first case of martyrdom occurred during these days: a child in Bucharest was tortured to death at the central police station.

The leadership of the Iron Guard saw that the victims were not showing signs of resistance, and the Leader of the State merely delivered a paternal slap on the wrist during a cabinet meeting; it was at this point that it was decided to commence with organized terror. An historical date was chosen for this purpose, one which held a long tradition for the Romanian police. The anniversary of the Russian Revolution had always provided an occasion for Jew-baiting. Around November 7 police and Iron Guard units went on patrol randomly arresting Jews that crossed their path. In Bucharest hundreds of Jews were dragged off to police cells or Iron Guard centers. The most horrifying torture centers were at the Bucharest Police Headquarters and the Iron Guard centers in Traian Street, Cercului Street and Roma Street. With neither pretext nor reason they tortured, tormented and mugged the incarcerated Jews, later releasing them to make room for new ones.

The catastrophic earthquake that struck the country the following night was not in the least perceived as a sign from heaven by those who had decorated their barbarity with mysticism and sanctimoniousness; on the contrary, it offered a fresh opportunity for persecution and terrorization. In Panciu, close to the epicenter of the quake, Jews were evicted from the ruins of their houses, and not one of them was allowed to return for four years.

In Bucharest, Jewish physicians who had offered their services to care for the injured were beaten and tortured by their Christian colleagues.

In Ploesti, the county head ordered the rounding up of all able-bodied Jews, from manual laborers to representatives of the intelligentsia, and forced them to carry out the strenuous task of clearing the debris. Jewish hands were forced to demolish almost all of the synagogues and a large fraction of Jewish cultural institutions. Terror was used to paralyze any attempt at resistance: the same county head turned a blind eye to the arrest of sixty Jews by the Iron Guard Chief of Police in the synagogue during service. They were tortured barbarically for two weeks. The victims of the Iron Guard night of revenge were selected from these Jews. While in Jilava the nation's high-ranking dignitaries who either spoke out or rose up against the madness of the Iron Guards were being slaughtered, in Ploesti eleven randomly selected Jews (headed by the community rabbi) were shot dead; their corpses were thrown into ditches along roads near the town. On that night Iron Guard hatred fused the pain of the Jews with the pain of the entire country. On the wooden floor of the Gendarme Legion building in Prahova—alongside Rabbi Filderman and Smuil Smilovici, the pretzel vendor—Nicolae Iorga, the apostle of Romanian culture, and indirectly that of anti-Semitic intolerance, also lost his life.

Alongside the threats, beatings, torture and murders aimed at intimidating the Jewish population, mass looting campaigns were initiated. Following the above-mentioned sporadic and minor acts of theft, and similar events in Aiud, Orastie and Turnu Severin, a large scale attack was launched. On November 16, after all Jewish religious and cultural institutions had been violently occupied, Iron Guard members in Brasov dragged a large number of Jewish merchants out of their shops, and demanded that they sign contracts of sale handing over Jewish businesses to "the Iron Guard Movement" or its members. All those who refused to sign were tortured until they did so.

This extremely swift campaign was almost a complete success. Within five days almost eighty per cent of Jewish businesses found their way into the hands of looters. The economic organization of the Saxons, the "Deutche

Handels Gremium zu Kronstadt" also made various attempts at looting, but were prevented by the vigilance of the Iron Guard.

In the wake of this easy victory, "the battle for Jewish businesses and property"—as it was referred to in official documentation—continued with increasing rage and violence, and spread to encompass the entire country. It started in Southern Transylvania, where the campaign had almost reached completion by the end of December (with the amazing exception of Timisoara),. and then continued in Oltenia, where it lasted until January 10, and later under the planning and supervision of the Economic Council headed by Garneata, encouraged and supported by the police force and administrative apparatus of Horia Sima, it spread throughout the country; by the time the Iron Guard revolt began, this campaign had already achieved almost all of its desired aims.

The intimidated, persecuted and partially impoverished Jewish population of the country, threatened primarily with the prospect of imminent and total annihilation had by this time no political organization, either inside or outside the country, on whose support they could rely.

After Nazi rule had spread from Brest to territories beyond the Vistula, and from Narvik to the Mediterranean Sea, at a time when the Wehrmacht had an increasingly firm foothold on Romanian territory, the Minority Treaty offered no protection whatsoever.

Romanian political parties showed understanding towards Jewish grievances only to the extent justified by election interests and political trends.

Traditional Jewish political organizations, i.e. the "Association of Romanian Jews" and the "Jewish Party" had been disbanded in 1938, when the dictatorship of King Charles II began.

Due to either a miracle or the skillfulness of its leaders, the Zionist Organization succeeded in retaining its legal status during Iron Guard rule, even until August 1942. Naturally, however, because of its function it could not act as an organization defending Jews within the country. It was forced to remain passive.

Community organizations, religious communities and their unions remained the only institutions burdened with the difficult task of easing the suffering, whilst unable to avert it.

Realizing the danger in advance, in May 1940 an attempt was made to create a strong central organization capable of conducting political activity, and at the same time able to provide social aid. The Union of Jewish Religious Communities operated for about one year on the initiative and energy of one individual, and was the only line of defense Jews had against the hatred mounted against them from all sides.

Naturally, during the Iron Guard reign of terror, when the executive and judicial authorities vanished completely, little could be expected from the activities of the Jewish leadership. It is true that they quickly established a relationship with the Leader of the State, and achieved certain concessions here and there, which—sporadically and fleetingly—alleviated Jewish suffering in certain places. However modest these concessions might have been, they were worth striving for incessantly. With a decreased staff and a poor budget challenging the indifference among Jews, which was just as dangerous as the hatred and rage on the opposing side, the Jewish leadership took up the fight against the Iron Guard system. This battle was unequal, on one side there was power, the club and the gun, on the other Jewish self-esteem and pride. Yet (at the expense of horrifying Jewish blood and property sacrifices), the latter triumphed during the first phase of Nazi persecution. The Iron Guard system drowned in blood and ashes, and the activity of the Jewish leadership was a contributory factor. /... /

The hundreds of reports describing the grievances and suffering affecting Jews in every corner of the land, and outlining the terror and horror introduced everywhere by the murderous and destructive Iron Guard regime, were not intended to cause a change of heart in the Leader of the State, but sufficed to give this overzealous man a clear picture of how the foundations of the state were crumbling and thus endangering his position. One such report—on December 9, 1940—catalogued four hundred crimes in thirty-five locations, prompting General Antonescu to issue the following directive: "It is the responsibility of the Ministry of the Interior, together with a member of the Iron Guard Forum, appointed by Mr. Sima, to immediately examine these cases. They should summarize their findings in a report, and deliver it to me without delay. Should the complaints prove justified, it is their sole responsibility to take immediate action to ensure that my promises to the citizens, and the Iron Guard's promises to me are not simply empty words. Should such cases occur in the future, I will not endlessly tolerate irregularities which turn the country upside-down. I am daily assured by the Minister of the Interior that everything is quiet, and nothing is happening. I am not defending the Jews, who are in great part to blame for the unfortunate events which have struck the country, however, as head of government, I cannot tolerate activities which compromise the consolidation I have introduced. For this I need calm and order. Some people's flippant activities are a daily hindrance to me. These people fail to understand how much damage they cause, both to the country and the Iron Guard movement. Lastly, I would like to ask for everybody's co-operation in exerting an influence on the Iron Guard—some through their positions of respect within the movement, and others through the weight of their position within the state apparatus (the Ministry of the Interior)—so that they will renounce methods which yield nothing and compromise everything. I would like General Petrovicescu to inform me in writing that he has taken note of this directive, and indicate the steps he has taken towards its immediate implementation."

This directive did not bring a change for the better. The opposite was true! One thread of the frayed rope linking the general to the Iron Guard Movement was torn. The Jewish leaders carried on with their campaign until the very last moment, thus contributing to the general's decision to scrap the institution of Officers of Romanianization, and to expel some of the leaders behind the reign of terror from top positions in public offices: the Minister of the Interior, the General Director of Internal Security and the Chief of Police of Bucharest. This move was the signal for the so-called "uprising", which brought mourning, wailing and destruction to Jews, while closing a hellish chapter in Jewish suffering.

Belief and conjecture claiming that between September 6, 1940 and August 23, 1944 General Antonescu was concerned with the increasingly desperate plight of Romanian Jews, that he wanted to take care of them, that he expressed feelings of good-will towards them, and that he worried about them, are false or even criminal.

Even more mistaken and criminal are the conclusions drawn from this premise culminating in the ridiculous assertion that through his actions the lives of some of Romania's Jews were saved. Naturally, those passing judgment on the basis of the obviously false and artificial mentality which prevailed throughout Europe for five years, namely, that whosoever saved the life of a Jew was a saint, are ready to find excuses, offer justification and propose absolution. Human intellect and conscience, free from fleeting influences, are aware of the eternal truth: he who tortures or kills an innocent or defenseless person is a villain. The always well-informed, General Antonescu began by tolerating aggressiveness, torture, robberies and murders committed against the Jewish population, which he could never accuse of anything other than that which was loudly and consistently proclaimed by national-socialist propaganda; and ended by initiating measures or issuing directives and orders which inevitably lead to the robbing and mass murder of this section of the population.

From among the 400,000 Jewish martyrs who perished on Romanian soil during the time of the Hitlerite nightmare, more than 250,000 rest on the conscience of General Antonescu.

General Antonescu, while provoking the revolt, which at that dangerous moment saved the Jews from annihilation, was not motivated by altruistic or humane interests in regarding the most wretched victims of Iron Guard rule.

He instigated the revolt because he needed it. ......

The general had to prove his strength, as Hitler had to on June 30, 1934.

It seems the general had wished to put an end to his relationship with Iron Guard bands as early as the beginning of December, immediately after the massacre in Jilava. There was no opportunity for this however, neither through the issuance of a decree on the dissolution of the Iron Guard police—because it would have been easy to bypass—nor at the outbreak of arguments provoked by him during negotiations with Iron Guard leaders, which first occurred at the meetings of the Council of Ministers, when he condemned, with hypocritical vehemence, crimes committed by the Iron Guard; he, who would give the order for similar actions less than a year later.

His decision was to become final on January 11, following the final meeting of the Council of Ministers of the Iron Guard government. The general's servile dependence, however, forced him to seek permission from his Fuhrer, or at least to strengthen his political position through yet another display of his trust. He rushed to Brechtesgaden and on January 14, complimented Hitler in the usual way, and—and with even greater haste—hurried back to the Romania.

His confidants prepared a series of measures, out of which two held crucial importance:

1. The abolition of the Committees for Romanianization; these committees were made up of Iron Guard robbers, who—for self-interest or purely for the sake of destruction—undermined the national economy.

2. The replacement of the main protagonists of Iron Guard terror: the Minister of the Interior, the General Director of the State Security Service and the Chief of Police of Bucharest.

From then on everything followed naturally. It lasted for one entire day and night. The capital of the country was sizzling with preparation. Meetings, demonstrations, singing and speeches—in front of the crowd or hidden behind microphones—cheering, booing, shouting and the dashing of cars and motorbikes (couriers usually used motorbikes), and ... arrests, the arrest of Jews. Both rival camps were preparing for attack and defense. The third could do no more than wait helplessly for the disaster to happen.

The battle did not last long. From around midday of the first day until midday of the second the rebels were allowed to roam freely; overturn some trams; burn some fuel tanks; even attack a few official buildings, and commit atrocities against soldiers. However, when the general decided to quash the revolt, all he needed was a few hours: it took him from 2.00 p.m. that day until that night to put an end to everything.

Great force was not needed. A few small, well-armed troops deployed at the right places, accompanied by some small armored cars, with strict orders to shoot at any suspicious person, took over the few Iron Guard pockets of resistance in quick succession, and following some gun battles succeeded in silencing them. The gunfire continued throughout the night sporadically up until 5.00 am, when Horia Sima, issued the surrender document from his hideout.

This was how the Iron Guard revolt ended in the northern quarter of the capital, in the environs of respected public buildings and the palaces of Romanian nobility.

There were casualties on both sides, broken windows, some damaged walls, one looted and burnt out public building, ruined public offices, some thousands of men, women and children with raised hands and bowed heads stumbling among soldiers in loathsome elongated marching columns. They signaled the end of the Iron Guard era, the beginning of which had been pathetically declared by Horia Sima not more than three weeks previously in his New Year's message.

The revolt took on an entirely different shape in the other half of the capital, where, as a consequence of chronic dilapidation, Jewish homes were crowded in on top of one another. Here, the bands did not have to battle against tanks, or soldiers' bullets, not even against the truncheons of policemen. All they had to fight here were the beaming eyes of pale faces, the pleas of parched lips, the tears of women and children, and occasionally a threshold or two which, for one brief moment, senselessly resisted the barbaric hatchets and pick-axes.

This was the part of the city most under threat, a fact well-known by those who did everything to instigate the revolt; in spite of this, no one took measures in time to save—if not the belongings—then at least the lives of the inhabitants. The result of this indifference or intent: almost 100,000 people were thrown into the paths of liberated beasts.

On the first indication of the revolt or even before, the Jewish quarters were flooded by bands of murderers and robbers. Starting from about midday on Tuesday, and continuing until the dawn of that Friday, long after the rebels had surrendered, Jewish property and lives were at the mercy of Iron Guard pistols, pick-axes and boots. For almost 70 hours a swarm of several thousand men, women and children were unable to occupy themselves with anything other than assault, destruction, arson, robbery and murder.

All quarters and all targets were attacked at the same time. A walk of a couple of hundred meters through any of the Jewish quarters on January 21, would have ended in the sight of a burning temple, and the horrifying disgusting spectacle of dancers circling the flames to the music of "the sacred Iron Guard youth" or "the Death detachment". Farther on, one would have noticed some Jews with pistols aimed at them being pushed and punched towards Iron Guard headquarters or a terror center; farther still there was a line of lorries: dozens of Jews were being taken to the abattoir, to Baneasa, Jilava, etc., where they were to be killed with terrible cruelty. Meanwhile, there was robbery and destruction all over Jewish streets, devoid of even minimal police protection. During these days suburbanites poured into the Jewish quarter, secure in the knowledge that they could satisfy their desire for Jewish goods without the fear of legal penalties. Who could have resisted the temptation of becoming instantly wealthy, when there was no resistance, and no fear of ever having to pay for one's crimes?

There was no risk of mistaking those of a certain ethnic origin for the purposes of robbery or torture; signs on the homes of non-Jews clearly read "robbers have no business here". The sign that averted bands was "Christian property". Meanwhile, volunteer denunciators from the mass of followers and those too shy to operate off their own bat pointed out Jewish shops or flats which could be safely attacked. During the pogrom, which lasted for three days, not one Christian household was inconvenienced: all of the victims were Jewish.

Psychologists state even more strongly than criminologists that criminals, independent of their inherited abnormality, at the moment of committing a crime completely lose their moral sense. Suppressed instincts inherited from their ancestors the gorillas or even more ancient monsters awake within them, and these alter not only the souls of these people but also their physical features. This is more likely to happen to an unrestrained band of criminals. Such a group—when it meets with no resistance; when it allows itself to be carried away by rage, greed and destruction; when it becomes intoxicated with a thirst for blood—is transformed into a barbaric mob capable of perpetrating the most appalling acts. This is the only possible explanation of how such a mass of violent animals was able to come to the forefront of a nation whose chief characteristic is meekness, and how they managed to execute such an horrendous pogrom in

Bucharest, the first in the series of horrifying acts committed by the fascist nations during World War II.

On January 24 military vehicles removed the heaps of stripped, mutilated and disfigured Jewish corpses from the outskirts of the city, while sorrowful groups of women and children examined the bodies at the collection depot to search for those who had gone missing, and those they would never see again. Meanwhile, the ruins of Jewish temples and houses were still smoking, and Baron Manfred von Killinger arrived in the capital city as the Romanian Ambassador of the Reich.

The first episode of Jewish suffering had drawn to a close, and Teutonic hatred had arrived to usher in the second.

Part 2. The Pogrom in Iasi

Historical Review

During the first week of the war started by Nazi Germany and its allies against the Union of the Soviet Socialist Republics, the most horrifying pogrom in the recent history of mankind was committed in Romania. The large number of victims, the barbaric methods of torture and killing, the immeasurable robbery and destruction, the active participation in the pogrom in Iasi of every representative of the administrative authorities entrusted with the protection of citizens' lives and property on a local level, signify the culmination of those evil efforts which had been poisoning the minds of Romanians for three quarters of a century; on a universal level, it opened history's most tragic chapter. It served as the sign giving the go-ahead for bloodbaths not only in Antonescu's Iron Guard dominated Romania but throughout Nazi, fascist Europe, which was to claim six million Jewish lives in the following three years.

By 1941 the Teutonic extermination of Jews had not yet begun. The plans for crematoriums and gas chambers were only rough sketches in the most inhumane minds ever to appear on the face of the earth. Therefore, Iasi, the horrifying symbol of persecution, robbery and bloodbaths has no equivalent; Odessa, Golta, Katyn, Kiev, Maidanek, Auschwitz, Belsen, etc. could be listed as comparisons, but Iasi preceded these by months or even years. If we were to look for parallels of sorts in the past we would have to turn back a large number of pages in the history books: we would have to take a giant leap back in time.

The roots of the pogrom in Iasi lie deep beneath the rotting system of Romanian pseudo-democracy. This was not an outbreak of isolated passions, neither was it some sort of momentary lapse of reason. It did not come about through autogenesis in the beastly depths of some criminally disposed beings. It did not start on "that Sunday", June 29, 1941; nor did it start three days earlier, when the first murders were committed; not on June 22, when the war broke out; nor on September 6—one year earlier—when Ion Antonescu and his Iron Guard came to power, not even on

December 27, 1938, when Charles II abandoned political hypocrisy, and left the fate of the country in the hands of the anti-Semitic government of Octavian Goga and A. C. Cuza. The roots of the pogrom in Iasi as well as the crimes, robberies and suffering inflicted up until August 23, 1944 can be found in the distant past, which—sometimes inadvertently, but in most cases intentionally—facilitated the uncurbed practice of spreading hostile propaganda as well as aiding tacitly tolerated incitement and an endless catalog of unpunished abuse.

The officially anti-Semitic form of government, which started in 1867 and exerted an unswerving influence for half a century, and which forced on the nation the introduction of one hundred and ninety-six laws limiting the rights of Jewish citizens: inhumane expulsions from villages; depriving people of their basic human rights (the right to citizenship, education, work, the right to occupy positions in the civil service, the right to undertake free-lance jobs, etc.); illegal expulsions; acts of hooliganism by the Anti-Semitic League; persecution during the war for a Greater Romania; Jewish regiments in the first front lines; the 1922 generation with its ominous moral and financial campaigns; disturbances and beatings at universities; the robbing and looting of Jewish synagogues and cemeteries; unpunished murders; Oradea, Borsa; the *Numerus Valahicus*; incitement in and expulsion from the Law Society; the Goga-Cuza government; the revival of an anti-Semitic form of government; the pogroms of June 1940; the jettisoning of Jews form moving trains; the legal status of Jews in August 1940; Antonescu and the Iron Guard system with its robberies and murders; discriminatory legislation, which raised the robbery and, finally, the Iron Guard revolt, which led to suffering and destruction, to the level of state dogma,—these were merely signposts on the endless road paving the way to annihilation.

Following these antecedents came World War II. As soon as the first day, or even before, the two Antonescus, along with their ministers and generals, decorated themselves with the wreathes of unremitting anti-Semitism, the leaves of which constituted a series of aggressive and oppressive measures. The eviction of Jews from small towns and villages, their cross-country transportation in closed freight cars under the pretext of ensuring the safety of territories behind the front line; the taking of Jewish, and exclusively Jewish, hostages, and their incarceration so that they could pay with their lives for any acts of terrorism or sabotage; the sticking up of millions of posters inciting people to kill Jews and communists; the removal of their legal protection by forcing them to wear the medieval yellow star. These were the Romania's fascist leaders following the outbreak of war. Their effect was not long coming. Under the skies of Romania an atmosphere of suspicion, contempt and hatred was activated against anything Jewish. The Jews of Iasi were the ones to experience this the most acutely.

In Iasi people's consciences had been saturated and devoured by this poison for more than three quarters of a century. In the hometown of Xenopol and Vasile Conta, Nicolia Ionescu, Ciaur Aslan, A. C. Cusa and Cornileu Codreanu, the bastion of the National Christian Defense League, the cradle of the Iron Guard movement, it was only natural that the microbes could find the most suitable culture-medium and the most prudent and unassuming in the country, and transform them into a mob simmering with hatred.

The geographical and strategic location of the town contributed to the mob's restlessness. Close to the front, 16 km from the river Prut, the inhabitants of Iasi were conscious of being within the firing range of Soviet cannons, and aware that they were easy targets for Soviet aircraft. In addition, the idea of the heavy and destructive fighting spreading to the areas surrounding the town, or to the town itself terrified them. When it became known that the German-Romanian attacks had been repelled by the skillfulness and courage of the Soviet infantry and armored divisions near the Sculeni abutment, the restlessness turned to panic.

Rumours, reports and alerts started to emanate from every local authority office—carefully rationed—attributing the shortcomings on the front line and the success of the Soviet air force, in control of the air-space over Iasi, to the town's Jews. Within a short period of time, the unaccountably large number of corps officers, warrant officers, police superiors and ordinary officers were suggesting to the entire population of the town that the Jews were transmitting information to the enemy by radio, and signaling to Soviet pilots—who were Jews from Iasi themselves anyway—with bulbs built into chimneys, or with linen and clothing hung on clothes lines, to let them know where the targets were and which ones to attack, and finally, that they were hiding and supporting Soviet parachutists who were preparing to occupy the town. The lunacy of this panic was complemented by the delirium of unbridled hatred. This was the moment when the signal for the pogrom was given.

The atrocities against the Jews, which began on Thursday afternoon and were repeated on Friday and Saturday morning, during which seven Jews were killed, many injured and several businesses looted and destroyed, subsequently culminated in the violence and destruction of the great pogrom, which began on Saturday night.

On that night, at around 9.00 p.m., following the signals from a German aircraft, heavy shooting started from guns and automatic weapons in almost every quarter of the town. At the same time, German and Romanian military patrols, ordinary policemen, solitary soldiers or civilians recruited from among the bourgeoisie, starting from the mob from pubs and dens all the way up to merchants, clerks, or intellectuals, forced their way into Jewish shelters and homes, carried out searches, tortured those inside, committed murders, and then collected most of the Jews, or at least every man, and dragged them to several collection sites. Most of the victims were taken to Police Headquarters, where by the morning 2,000 people were crammed, the number rising to 5-6,000 by midday, as a result of the continuous influx of new arrivals.

All day on Sunday, until twilight, those dragged to Police Headquarters were beaten and tortured with unprecedented cruelty. In the end, roughly one third of them were murdered. Without pity, shots were fired from all kinds of weapons into the group of people wailing with fear and pain. Pistols, carbines and automatic guns were positioned in front of them or behind them in the yard of Police Headquarters, at the doors and windows of the building as well as in neighboring property. The torture and murder was carried out with the passive participation of all the military and civil authorities.

Everybody was there, from army division commander and county head to the last sergeant of the Gendarmerie or police officer...

Simultaneously with the bloodbath organized in the yard of the Police Headquarters, a great number of Jews were killed on Sunday in flats, cellars, yards and in the streets. The slaughter in the streets continued into the second or even third day.

On the same night, on the initiative of local military authorities, and with the approval of senior governmental bodies, the approximately 4,500 survivors were taken in marching columns, amid barbaric acts of torture, to the railway station and put on two trains for the purposes of evacuation and internment in Podul Iloaiei and Targu Frumos, in the same county.

They were crammed in overcrowded carriages (at times as many as one hundred and fifty people in one box car), the doors were shut and, in many cases, even sealed, the vents were stuffed, there was no food, little air and no water, and they were fired upon any sudden movement. Consequently, almost two thirds of the evacuees died during the journey.

The exact number of the victims of the pogrom in Iasi will never be known. Even if this figure did not reach 12,000, as is believed by many, it is definitely over half of this number. During the trial, the number was put at 8,000.

Naturally, the fascist judiciary of the time did not take one single step to punish the beasts guilty of so many crimes. From among Antonescu's countless military and civilian judges and prosecutors—who had not hesitated to sentence to death workers who, for one day, failed to show up for slave labor in "the public interest", or children who dared believe in a better future—not one could be found who, formally at least, would have been prepared to initiate legal proceedings for the purposes of punishing those responsible for the Iasi bloodbath.

One of the first initiatives of the democratic faction of the Romanian government after August 23 (August 23, 1944, the day Romania switched sides) was concerned with the punishment of war criminals; the first among them were those who had prepared, organized and executed the pogrom in Iasi. However, the tireless efforts of Romanian democracy came up against obstacles to justice and jurisdiction laid in the their path by the last remnants of fascist reactionary forces. Serious crimes concerning the highest circles prevented the People's Jury from fully carrying out its tasks. Wrapped in their crimson cloaks, these people were able to scheme and procrastinate freely in the labyrinth of legal volumes for almost three years.

It was only in June 1948 (...) that the sentencing of those responsible could commence with sincere intentions.

Fifty seven defendants were summoned before the Criminal Court (which included three people's judges) to answer for their terrible deeds; these included a general, formerly the commander of an army corps, and five colonels. The morally immaculate hearing continued for nearly two weeks, during which time the accused were unable to refute the incontrovertible evidence the prosecuting magistrate, whose aim it was to expose the entire truth, had gathered against them.

The final chapter of this tragedy ended with a sentence which was as much deliberated as it was just and severe.

Initiative, Organization and Aims

From among the awkward tasks faced by researchers investigating the web of lies, insidiousness, greed and murder that constituted the pogrom in Iasi, the most delicate is that aimed at revealing the full truth concerning the initiative that sparked off this hell. The barbaric deeds committed in broad daylight or under the cover of darkness were seen, heard and felt by a community of more than one hundred thousand. Most members of this community—victims, murderers, thieves and onlookers—have survived the events and the years since then. We have an abundance of tales, which are usually similar. By evaluating them we can come up with a picture of the train of events during the pogrom not much removed from the truth.

The initiative, however, as well as the devilish plans were agreed upon behind padded and closed doors. Few people were members of the evil caucuses, and even fewer would like to unravel the truth today. Therefore, we cannot solely rely on the tangible world of facts and documentation; the truth must be extracted from the muddled confusion of assumptions, which are nevertheless underpinned by the evidence forced out of those who had tried to remain silent in vain.

Whether or not the Romanian leadership was aware of this initiative is debatable, and if it was, then to what extent, neither do we know whether or not it agreed with it, and once again, if so, then to what extent. However, an order of general bearing containing one of the shameful directives issued by Ion Antonescu on June 19 seems to support the idea that he had been informed. This view is also backed up by the incessant anti-Semitic hatred expressed and propagated by the country's leaders during the first days of the war. Finally, this question is answered by their unreserved approval, which manifested itself in the mindless decrees issued by Ion Antonescu himself immediately following the bloodbaths on July 1 and 2, 1941.

For the civilized human being the aims of the organizers of the bloodbath are obscure and incomprehensible. If it is true that it had been organized by the Germans, then it would appear that they were aiming for a display of strength intended to generate fear and respect in Romanian masses and leaders, and to maintain the inferiority complex which had been characteristic of Romanian-German co-operation from the outset.

The Romanian and German secret services and police had been entrusted with the preparation and organization of the pogrom in Iasi. The SSI (Serviciul Special de Informatiuni—the Special Information Service), consisting of a network of secret agents and criminals, was considered to be especially capable of carrying out this task.

Romanian reactionary forces had always made ample use of the benefits provided to an oligarchic political system by a despised police force—especially during the period between the two world wars. The reputation for persecution of the Police Chief Administration, which had belonged to the Ministry of the Interior, the notorious Siguranta, will remain among those organizations of great renown, i.e. the Czarist Ochrana, the British Intelligence Service or the German Gestapo. For decades it suppressed all drives towards freedom and development with terror and torture, imprisoned working people and martyrs, who had fought for a better life. However, when the royal dictatorship started to interfere in the governing of the country, and especially when it openly seized power, the Siguranta, with its links to political parties, was no longer fit for the purposes of executive power. Therefore, the King decided to establish his own police force. At first, this was a small nucleus consisting of a tiny group of people led by the Palace Marshal, who slowly developed it further. This is how the Special Information Service (SSI), the police force involved in internal espionage, the activities of which were directed against politicians, communists and co-existing ethnic groups, came into existence.

Following the expulsion of Charles II, this weapon of terror, formerly the property of the royal dictatorship, was inherited by the fascist Iron Guard dictatorship. The Palace Marshal was watchful enough to retain it for himself. He gave the Iron Guard members a free hand in wreaking revenge, which culminated in the bloodbath in Jilava on November 17, 1940, during which, among others, the former heads of the SSI, Mihail Moruzov and Niky Stefanescu were assassinated. He even allowed them to establish their own police force, the horrifying Iron Guard Police, an institution of torture, robbery and murder. He did not, however, allow his political friends to lay their hands on the SSI. Shortly after his inauguration on November 11, 1940, Antonescu attached the entire SSI system to his cabinet, and appointed one of his confidantes, Eugen Critescu, as its head, who proved very competent, and loyally served his master. The SSI network soon encompassed the capital and the provinces, and set up its foreign information service. In Bucharest a few hundred Jews were evicted from their flats to provide the SSI with an entire street inaccessible to strangers. A large number of senior officers were redeployed to the innumerable departments of the Special Service. In the provinces, agencies known as residencies were organized; their sphere of activities included the observation of Jews and communists, and the filing of names for use at an appropriate time in the future.

The activities of the SSI were also assisted by the Second Head Department of the General Command headed by Colonel Radu Dinulescu, as well as an enormous number of former Iron Guard members and informers, whose anti- Semitism would pass any test.

Either with or without the permission of the SSI, the General Command and the Siguranta Center, another enormous espionage network, and secret police operated on Romanian soil at the time: this belonged to the German Reich. The provision for impunity following acts of provocation and anarchy, and the intrusion of the so-called fifth column into every aspect of the political and economic landscape were among the considerable achievements of German Secret Service activities, and especially those of the Gestapo.

Simultaneously with the arrival of German troops in the country, there was a proliferation of secret Nazi espionage organizations and military or political services in the autumn of 1940.

While the archives of the SSI remained untouched, files referring to the bloodbath in Iasi were immediately after August 23, or perhaps a little later, either hidden or destroyed. Only the files belonging to the Ministry of the Interior and the Gendarmerie General Inspectorate are at the disposal of history and justice. These files, however, contain only a few details about the course of events during the pogrom.

Therefore, the preparations for the pogrom in Iasi can be reconstructed only on the basis of evidence and individual testimonies collected by judicial bodies. However, these are also incomplete, since the testimonies of Germans and deceased Romanians are missing. Also missing is the testimony of General von Schobert - who died in an aviation accident near Kiev; and the testimonies of Generals von Hauffe and Gerstenberg, who headed the German military mission in Romania; no evidence was given by General von Salmuth, Commander of the XXX German Military Corps; nor by General von Roetig, Commander of the 198th Army Division; nor by Colonel Rodler, the Romanian head of the Abwehr; nor by his right-hand man, Alexander von Stransky; nor from Captain Hoffman, commander of the German garrison in Iasi; and absent above all others is the testimony of Baron Manfred von Killinger, German Ambassador to Bucharest. Similarly missing are the testimonies of certain Rumanian personalities, the most important of whom are: Becescu-Georgescu, the Director of the SSI—who died a few years ago; Major Emil Tulbure, representative of the SSI in Iasi, who died of a heart attack a few days after the pogrom; his assistant, Major Gheorghe Balotescu, who disappeared in Germany after August 23, 1944. From the testimonies and documents at our disposal we can, nevertheless, pick out certain elements which enable us to reconstruct the prologue to the pogrom.

From these it turns out that before the start of military operations, upon the orders of Ion Antonescu and General Headquarters, the so-called SSI Mobile Detachment No.1 was formed with the acknowledged aim of combatting espionage, sabotage and terrorist actions, and with the secret aim of organizing anti-espionage, anti-sabotage and anti-terrorist actions.

The detachment consisted of about 160 persons selected from among the most able, courageous and reliable people in the SSI. Among the members of the detachment were: Eugen Cristescu, the all-powerful director; his right hand man, Colonel Ion Lisievici, Head of the Information Department; Lieutenant-Colonel Constantin Ionescu Micandru, Head of Department "G", which provided contact with the Germans; his inseparable shadow, the German Major Herman von Stransky; Lieutenant-Colonel Proca Alexandru, Head of the Anti-Sabotage Department; Director Florin Becescu-Georgescu, Head of the Counter-Espionage Department. In addition to these people, members of the detachment included the bravest agents and group leaders: Gheorghe Critescu (brother of Eugen Critescu), Grigore Guta Petrovici, Teodor Rosianu (alias Relu Critescu) and many more.

The detachment set off in cars towards Bessarabia on June 18, 1941. Upon leaving, Director Florin Becescu-Georgescu took the pre-prepared charts and files indicating the geographical location of the Jewish population. After resting for short periods in Maia, near Snagov, and Vartejcoiu, near Odobesti, and somewhat longer periods in Vadu, near Piatra Neamt and Soprocesti, near Roman, the detachment arrived in Iasi.

Then they continued on their way leaving blood and ruins in their wake in Kishinew, Tighina, Tiraspol, Odessa, and all the way to Rostow.

Throughout the journey the detachment kept in constant contact with the various agencies and residencies, especially the one in Iasi. The heads of the residencies in Iasi, Majors Emil Tulbure and Gheorghe Balotescu, received instructions and commands telling them when to start work. It is not out of the question that the directives were forwarded by Colonel Lisievici, or Lieutenant-Colonel Proca, the head of the Anti-Sabotage Department. It is certain that plans and orders concerning the job were passed on to them by Lieutenant-Colonel Ionescu Micandru and Major Stransky, so that they could supervise events more closely.

Major Stransky and Lieutenant-Colonel Ionescu Micandru hurried to Iasi on June 26, spent a few hours at the Headquarters of 14th Division, and then left the town in the evening disappearing mysteriously, probably heading for the village of Bucium, where the SSI Representatives were accommodated.

The Representatives were now able to report to their superiors that they had recruited, trained and armed about thirty or forty Iron Guards, who were staying in a flat rented by a lawyer in Florilor St. in the Pacurari quarter. As a matter of fact, they were found there the following day by Colonel Constantin Lupu, the garrison commander who—although he had arrived there as a result of a very serious complaint to the police—succumbed to orders coming from above, and would not in any way hinder them in the course of events to come.

They were also in a position to inform Lieutenant-Colonel Micandru that Iron Guard member Mircea Manoliu, who had been called up as a reserve lance-sergeant in the zone of the 13th Dorobanti Regiment, was given the task of carrying out blatant acts of terrorism in order to experiment on the reactions of the authorities who had not been informed of the preparations in advance. On the same night, Manoliu fired at three Jews killing only one; the following night he killed another six, and on Saturday morning he incited the Abattoir quarter to robbery, and the mob on the outskirts to atrocities.

The organizers of the pogrom had no further reasons for indecision. By this stage, they could be sure of success, and only the final orders remained to be given.

The Iron Guard mercenaries were deployed to occupy various positions in every quarter of the town. They were well-equipped with low caliber weapons, defense guns[1], and blank bullets, which were only meant to make noise. Many of them, however, possessed lethal weapons, and fired them without pity at the unfortunates who were trying in vain to hide.

The Teutonic brigades were also alerted, and they too set off, with some of them provoking, and others killing. Their patrols were ready to break into previously marked Jewish houses while giving the impression of being attacked. The crosses painted on houses and fences did not really interest them, because they knew that in this poisoned town they had the looting-hungry mob at their disposal, and that the mob would point out the houses to be attacked.

---

1   .22 caliber rifle used in pre-military training.

They also warned representatives of the authorities whom they had informed of their plot in time, and who issued their final instructions, e.g. Police Captain Leahu ordered police officers not to interfere with what the army was doing, irrespective of whether it was right or wrong.

From the headquarters of the Mobile Detachment, Major Gheorghe Balotescu summoned his close friend, "Inspector" Grigore Petrovici, who hurried to Iasi with his entire unit.

Finally, one last instruction to the anti-aircraft defense service, that within the overall scheme of the pogrom their task was to sound false air-raid sirens twice, at set times.

Saturday, 9.30 p.m., June 28, 1941. The "H" hour!... One siren, one aircraft, one rocket. All hell broke loose.

The Chronological Order of Events

June 19 - July 6, 1941

June 19, 1941

The issue of going to war against the Soviet Union had already been decided, and the preparations had been laid for its outbreak. Antonescu had been informed of the devilish secret in January; in the months that followed, the country's high-ranking civil and military leaders were also brought into the picture; the ordinary people had started to sense it during the last few days. Nobody doubts the ensuing danger.

Final preparations are taking place everywhere.

Ion Antonescu orders the Ministry of the Interior to observe Jews with increased alertness, and to count their numbers in every province so that "action can be taken against them when I order it, and when the suitable time comes".

The Ministry of the Interior gives the orders by telephone to immediately evacuate the Jewish citizens from villages and towns in Moldova - the men

to Targu Jiu, women, children and the elderly to county centres; the orders
are confirmed in writing a few days later. Orders are also issued by telephone to arrest large groups of Jews in every town. They will be forced to
give their lives for any acts of aggression, sabotage or terrorism that may occur. The orders were executed with fanatical relentlessness and relentless
fanaticism.

General Headquarters sets off towards the Prut, followed closely by the 1st
Mobile Detachment of the Special Information Service executing its
damned, secret missions. Documents and files on Jews prepared earlier by
the SSI were hidden among the detachment's equipment.

June 22, 1941

The war starts. Romanian leaders begin stirring up anti-Semitic hatred on
the first day. Posters of all sizes and colors are stuck up everywhere: on
fences, kiosks, trams, train carriages and walls (especially the walls of public
offices), calling for pogroms against Jews, and blaming them for the war.

Throughout the country, from Moldova to Oltenia, trains depart with
sealed freight wagons packed with thousands of Jews. These starving and
thirsty men, women, children and old people were grabbed from their
homes, robbed of their possessions, and forced towards the terrible concentration camps of Targu Jiu, Craiova, Caracal, Turnu Severin, Lugos,
etc.

In Iasi, where the number of Jews is high, anti-Semitic hatred is even
greater than in any other part of the country.

June 24, 1941

The first Soviet air attack; bombs are dropped on the Rapa Galbena district
of town and on the station. The damage caused by the bombs was minimal, but the panic among people was immense. This atmosphere of panic
served to strengthen the alarming rumors spreading fom military and Iron
Guard circles, and gave weight to accusations laid against Jews in
Iasi—and Jews everywhere—who were accused of being in league with Soviet pilots; that they had showed which targets were to be bombed, and

that the pilots of the Soviet planes were also Jews from Iasi. All this created a state of collective lunacy, and almost the entire population of Iasi was transformed into a frightened mob, which unthinkingly considered the Jews its greatest threat.

11.00 hrs, June 26, 1941

The second Soviet blitz. Targets bombed included the Headquarters of the 14th Division, the Central Telephone Exchange and the Saint Spiridon Hospital. Many dead, of whom 38 were Jewish.

June 26, 1941

In Iasi's evening newspaper (*Prut*), General Gheorghe Stavrescu, the Commander of the 14th Infantry Division, the highest-ranking local military officer, issues a warning, in which, among other things, he asks people to help the authorities catch "our enemies and spreaders of alarming rumors", and threatens that, "those in the service of the enemy will be hacked to pieces". The newspaper was dated June 27, but taking into consideration the usual system of dating newspapers, it probably appeared on June 26.

......

Jewish citizens Isoub Cojocaru, Leon Schachter and Wolf Herscu (the latter seriously injured during the morning's Soviet bomb attack), who live next to the building where the batteries of the 13th Dorobanti Regiment were accommodated, are accused of giving signals from their flats to the Soviet air force, and escorted to the headquarters of the regiment by Lance-Sergeant Mircea Manoliu. Once there they are interrogated by two captains—well-disposed people—who give an order to let them go free, because they found the arrested men entirely innocent. Since the headquarters are in the district called Copou, in which Jews are forbidden to move, the officers order Lance-Sergeant Manoliu to accompany them, for their safety, until they are outside the danger zone. Mircea Manoliu, however, does not take them back along the short route by which they came, instead, he takes a detour through the narrow, empty streets heading towards the shooting ground in Calcaina valley. When no one is watching, the beast shoots the people he is supposed to be guarding. Cojocaru dies immediately, the seriously injured Wolf Herscu falls unconscious, but Schachter, who was not hit, manages to escape and hide in the corn field.

June 27, 1941

A few kilometres from the above scene, in Sculeni, there is a terrible massacre; it is the prelude to the tragedy planned for Iasi. The conquerors found themselves facing the heroic resistance of the Red Army. Slyly and using an element of surprise, they managed to build a small, abutment 5 kilometres deep, on the eastern side of the Prut. Two battalions of the German 305th Regiment commanded by Colonel Buck were encamped there, as was another battalion (commanded by Major Garaiac) of the 6th Mountain Rifle Regiment (under the command of Colonel Ermil Maties). The officers of this cursed battalion (which speckled the road from Sculeni to Odessa with dead bodies) turned to German Headquarters and requested to be directed to this district so as to be able to take revenge on the Jews who had supposedly humiliated them when they withdrew in 1940.

Hardly had the three battalions settled down in Soviet territory, than an attack by Soviet infantrymen, supported by tanks, drove back the two German battalions. Only the Romanian battalion held its position, and within its ranks the commander squadron of the 6th Rifle Regiment headed by two officers in contact with German Central Command, Captain Ion Stihi and Sub-Lieutenant Eugen Mihailescu. These two circulate false information that the Romanian failure as well as the German withdrawal occurred because they had been attacked by the Jews of Sculeni. The Commander of the Military Sector, the German Colonel Buck, deploys new German battalions, and re-occupies previously controlled trenches. He then orders the evacuation of the civil population from Targu Sculeni.

Christian citizens were directed to the villages of Carlig and Copou, the poor Jews, however, who had been driven to Stanca Rosnoveanu, found themselves under the control of the two beasts—Captain Stihi and Sub-Lieutenant Mihailescu. Both of them were natives of the area (the theology student Mihailescu was the son of the town-clerk of Sculeni), both were members of the Iron Guard, and both were greedy and brimming with hatred. They forced 40 men to dig four holes long and wide, and before killing every Jew in Sculeni with their own hands, they threw all the gold they found on the Jews into a tent sheet; there was only a Lance-Sergeant and a private (originally a butcher) to help them.

In September 1945 the graves were opened; in three of the four holes the corpses of 311 Jews were found, including 7 babies, 38 children under the age of twelve, 46 children under the age of eighteen and 91 women. The skeletons of several children lay as they were at the time of death —embracing the necks of their mothers.

The mass-murder in Stanca Rosnoveanu was ordered by high-ranking officers; Commander of the 6th Mountain Rifle Regiment, Colonel Ermil Maties, was among those who issued the command. Not only does he freely admit this, but also cynically apologizes for committing "too few" crimes against the Jews of Sculeni.

The curators of the religious community and the leaders of the Jewish citizens are summoned to appear at the Central Police Office by Lieutenant-Colonel Constantin Chirilovici, the delegated Police Superintendent. In the name of the Commander of the Army, who could have been none other than General Gheorghe Stavrescu, he accuses the Jewish population of co-operating with the Soviet air force, and, using very strong language, calls upon Jews to "return to legal ways"; he threatens to kill 100 Jews for every Romanian or German soldier killed. Finally, he orders Jews to turn in all their telescopes, flashlights, cameras and film.

June, 27 1941

A meeting is held in the County Office. The participants:

Colonel Dumitru Captaru, county head; Colonel Constantin Lupu, garrison commander; Lieutenant-Colonel Constantin Chirilovici, Police Superintendent; Giosanu and Cosma, State Security Inspectors; the Attorney-General (probably Ion Aburel), and the chief medical officer of the town. They decide to establish a Gendarme district to work alongside each police district; the officers leading these Gendarme districts will help catch snipers, even though not one single suspicious shot has been fired anywhere. Colonel Lupu states that this meeting took place on June 27, but adds that on the day of the bombing (which means it took place on

June 26) General Leoveanu, the ex-senior director of the State Security (Siguaranta) Office, who was sent to Iasi by Antonescu on July 2 to investigate the disturbances which took place there, states—based on the press release of Lieutenant-Colonel C. Chirilovici, Police Superintendent—that the decision to implement these measures was made on the morning of June 28.

June 27, 1941

The Police Superintendent informs the Commander of the Garrison by phone that a group of Iron Guards gathered in the Pacurari. district are singing Iron Guard marching songs, and rabble-rousing. When Colonel Lupu arrives on the scene with a platoon, he finds about thirty or forty armed Iron Guards led by two officers in civilian clothing: Majors Gheorghe Balotescu and Emil Tulbure. Two crates of weapons are also found in the pavilion. The Commander of the Garrison does no more than ascertain the facts, and fails to take any further action. He returns to Headquarters, where within an hour the two majors also appear; they show the papers they received from General Headquarters, and say that they had intended to operate under cover, but had not been successful.

Lieutenant-Colonel Traian Borcescu, a secretary at the Special Information Service (SSI), states that the two majors personally participated in the preparations for the massacre in Iasi, and adds that apart from them the following SSI members were also involved in the massacre: Grigore Petrovici, Gheorghe Cristescu (Eugen Cristescu's brother), under the command of Director Florin Becescu-Georgescu.

June, 27, 1941

The atmosphere in Iasi becomes more and more depressing, all activity is paralyzed. A large number of Christian intellectuals and wealthy people leave Iasi. Many Christian houses are marked with a cross. Some kindly-disposed Christians warn their friends to leave town.

June 27-28, 1941 (at night)

The soldiers of the 13th Guardsmen Division arrest six more Jews on charges of espionage. They are sent to Headquarters escorted by the same Lance-Sergeant, Mircea Manoliu, who on the previous day shot dead two of the three Jews in his charge. This time Manoliu did not wait until they had reached Headquarters. He took his victims on a long detour leading to the abattoir. Manoliu and his escort, Corporal Nicolau, killed all six Jews with bullets from their carbines and pistols. There may only have been five of them, since this is the number to which Manoliu confesses. Back with his corps, this criminal justified his action with the classic lie that the Jews had wanted to escape and that was why he had killed them. It is possible that this beast had committed this crime, as well as that of the previous day, of his own accord as a consequence of the atmosphere of hostility present in the town. If we consider that the killer was a well-known Iron Guard from Bivolar, we can suppose that the Iron Guard organizers of the pogrom had encouraged him to gauge the standpoint and potential reactions of the authorities. Therefore, Manoliu's crimes represent the first episode of the Iasi pogrom, not only from a chronological, but also from an organizational viewpoint.

10.00 hrs, June 28, 1941

Under the leadership of the same Lance-Sergeant Mircea Manoliu, the soldiers of the 13th Guardsmen Regiment, the 24th Artillery Regiment and the 14th Ammunition Transportation Regiment, joined by a German military unit and the local residents of Aurel Vlaicu Street, harass and rob Jews in the Abattoir district under the pretext of searching for radio transmitters. The Police Superintendent, the Commissioner of the Garrison (the latter with a brigade of policemen), the Attorney-General of the Court of Justice and the military judge of the 14th Division arrive at the scene of the crimes, state the facts, but do not take any actions to punish the vandalism or prevent a repeat of similar actions. Moreover, Mircea Manoliu, the instigator of the murders, is immediately arrested, but released soon after by Major Nicolae Scriban, the military judge of the 14th Division. This was considered, even by the Antonescu-authorities, as an action, which could have serious consequences. Consequently, General Ion Topor, the then Highest Military Judge, sentenced Major Scriban to ten days in prison.

The authorities order a Gendarme to be sent to every police district. Some hours later, on the night which witnessed the beginning of the bloodshed, reconnaissance units as well as groups of robbers and killers emerge from among these.

June 28, 1941

Police Superintendent Gheorghe Leahu orders police officers to surrender their weapons. A few hours later this order is withdrawn, but a further order issued on the same day by Leahu calls on policemen not to intervene in "what the army is about to do, regardless of the rights or wrongs of their actions".

June 28, 1941

Siguaranta (Security Service) and police groups arrest a large number of Jews because they are either considered left-wing sympathizers, or their names are marked as "suspicious elements" for other actions in police files. All of them are locked up in the basement of the Central Police Station.

21.00 hrs, June 28, 1941

A false air-raid alarm. Only a few German planes appear, a blue flare is fired from one of them. This was the signal for the pogrom. The shooting started immediately in every district of the town, with pistols and machine guns, firstly, in the districts of Pacurari, Toma Cosma and Sararie, and also in Carol Street. Shots were fired in the streets from houses, from the attic of the University, from Saint Spiridon Hospital, from the building of the State Archives Office, etc. Shots were fired into the air, but also at people, at the troops marching towards the front. Many shots were fired at a column of Romanian soldiers, who were marching towards Lascar Catargiu Street, and at another column marching along Carol Street and Laspusneanu Street. The latter went into a state of complete disarray, took up battle positions, and opened fire with every type of weapon, even 53 millimetre cannons.

Even though the shooting bore all the features of genuine battle, not one soldier was killed or injured, no weapons were found anywhere, and not one single marksman was arrested from one single house.

...

The Germans, however, tried to pretend that there were dead and injured among their ranks. The public both believed and exaggerated the German version of events. High-ranking Romanian personalities, especially Colonel Captaru, the county head, allowed themselves to be deceived, or rather wanted to be deceived. Consequently, the authorities looked on the events as if the disturbance had been provoked by the Jews, and instead of acting against the criminals, they continued to encourage, actively and passively, those who had arranged the massacre.

Simultaneously with the shootings—which continued all night long—German guardsmen, who had checked the entire area of the town, forced their way into Jewish houses, exclusively Jewish houses, where, under the pretext of carrying out house-to-house searches, they arrested, assaulted, looted and murdered. Stationary and mobile Romanian patrols (which had been set up at the garrison), and individual soldiers as well as a large number of civilians also joined them. Policemen were members of other groups which searched houses. These marched out after being commanded to do so by the Central Police Station. The house searches were ordered by General Stavrescu, Commander of the 14th Division. If the inhabitants were not to be found in their flats (there was an air-raid alarm), the patrols forced their way into air-raid shelters.

June 29, 1941

Those who avoided the lethal bullets, are driven to the town centre. The never-ending marching columns arrive from every district of the town—mostly men, but there are also women and children: parents and children, grandparents and grandchildren, wives and husbands; some dressed, but in ragged clothes, others in pajamas; many barefoot; almost all bearing the marks of the previous night's injuries; with bruises, open wounds, tracks of blood, tears and sweat on their dirty faces. Despite being physically exhausted, they are forced to march in rhythmic steps. This is forced on them by the beasts. Most terrible of all; they have to keep their hands in the air at all times; they are forbidden to whisper, and death-threats discourage them from disobedience. They push and shove one another because everyone would like to be in the middle of the column, in the hope that there they would find brief refuge from the sticks of the mob standing by the roadside, wild with hatred and energized by the cruelty of the spectacle. They hope that the stones and mucus will not reach them, because they are insulted, spat at and beaten continually. This is how the Jewish columns made their way from the districts of Tatarasi, Paacurari, Sararie, Nicolina, from everywhere, among the dead bodies lying on the streets, in front of the ruined and plundered shops; the suppressed cries of the tortured are lost in the cacophony, in which the roaring of the mob and the constant rattle of firearms mingles with the tunes of waltzes coming from the loud-speakers of the German automobiles crisscrossing through the town.

Almost all the marching columns are driven towards the Central Police Station. A few, however, are led into the National Grammar School, the 13th Guardsmen Regiment, the Wachtel School and the County Office of the Security Service. These are later brought to the Central Police Office, the enormous yard of which will soon be too narrow for the thousands of people crowded there. Official reports mention 1,800-2,000 people at 9 o'clock in the morning, by noon 3,000-4,000, and according to some reports, as many as 5,000. Eye-witnesses, however, estimate the number to be in the region of 6,000. These people are waiting in fear for someone from the ranks of the powerful or the authorities swarming around the gate and the offices to decide their fate.

The previous night, General Stavrescu, Commander of local military forces (14th Infantry Division), the highest ranking local officer, had been informed of the forthcoming event by Captain Dane, Commander of the police squadron from the division, and the civilian police organizations. In spite of all this, he does not take any measures, does not report anything to higher authorities, and moreover, gives an order to search Jewish homes and arrest Jews. In his report, written two days after the events of that night, containing the insulting expression "Jewish-communist suspects", he reports that "those found guilty were executed there and then by Romanian-German forces.

"On that Sunday", General Stavrescu visited the Central Police Office several times. He even delivered a speech at 1100 hrs, which, although reassuring, did not omit the usual insulting expressions and threats. After the General had left, a committee was formed (at his request, it seems). Members included police officers Dimitru Iancu and Rahoveanu Titus, and Captain Dane, Commander of the division's police squadron. These pretended to make a selection of the arrested people, and 200 randomly chosen prisoners were set free without investigation; each of them was given a note saying that they were "Free". The notes were stamped by the Central Police Office. It cannot be stated categorically whether or not these notes were used as a ploy to trap the other Jews. What is sure is that the news spread quickly, and more Jews—much more than those who had been set free—came out of their hiding places, and went voluntarily to get these notes. However, once at the Central Police Office, they were not allowed to leave. They had volunteered in vain, and were forced to go to that cursed yard, between the rows of German beasts armed with sticks and iron bars, who beat them with such cruelty that a few of them dropped dead after the first blow.

General Stavrescu claims that on the occasion of his first visit to the Central Police Station, the Germans were already in control. However—even though there were two platoons of Gendarmes and a divisional police squadron under his command—it did not occur to him for a moment that he should safeguard the rights and sphere of activity of the Romanian authorities. Actually, there is no report, account or announcement to justify the claim that German forces actually and violently had taken over the Central Police Station. Police Superintendent Leahu did not elaborate further but said that the Germans had a unit of the Todt-Corps stand guard at the gate; Lieutenant-Colonel Police Superintendent Chirilovici, in one of his announcements of July 2, 1941, mentioned that there were a lot of German officers in the Central Police Station, who were witnesses to the events occurring there, but did not interfere in any way. General E. Leoveanu, the then director of the Siguranta (the State Secret Service), who was sent to Iasi to officially investigate the massacre, arrived before the pogrom had ended, and accused the commander of the garrison of not having taken the necessary measures to limit the bloodshed. Consequently, the Germans, if they had been there, could have been asked to leave.

The rumor that the Germans had occupied the Central Police Station was spread when the People's Tribunal launched its investigation; when the defendants—who had been decorated with stripes, braids and medals—instead of accepting responsibility for their gruesome sins, admitted that they themselves had felt under threat and as a result had behaved in a cowardly fashion.

At a specified time the selection of Jews was stopped, and new groups of arrestees were brought to the Central Police Station; among them were many of those who had previously been selected as prisoners to be freed. These horrifying acts continued until 1500 hrs, when the massacre proper started.

The signal for this was given through another false air-raid alarm. As the sirens began to screech, bullets were fired on the unfortunate people. The crowd of several thousand was shot at from all directions by pistols, guns and machine-guns: at the steps leading to the police station, from the gates, from the windows of the Central Police Station, from balconies of neighboring buildings and from rooftops. Those, who wanted to escape by climbing the fence that separated Union Square from the Central Police Station (Alecsandri Alley, the garden of the Sidoli cinema), were also shot. The army was prepared for this eventuality and closed off a circle around the streets of Vasile Alecsandri, Cuza Voda and Bratitanu as well as Union Square. The soldiers forced their way into houses, pulled out Jews and shot them dead on the spot.

Reports of the time are silent about this most awful part of that awful day. Only Lieutenant-Colonel Chirilovici, Police Superintendent, mentions it in his report. He tried to justify the massacre by saying that the soldiers were angered when local Jewish communists started firing at them because they wanted to free the Jews who had been arrested.

Those who survived the terrible massacre in the neighboring streets were taken to the building of the Gendarme Legion; there they had to stand with their hands held above their heads while soldiers beat them with sticks in full view of the officers. In the evening all of them were taken back to the yard of the Central Police Station, where they also met the fate of the others.

On that day, June 29, 1941, which is remembered as "that Sunday", scenes of mindless abuse, torture, looting and murder were played out before the indifferent eyes of those who represented Romanian civil and military authorities. Let us list them: General Gheorghe Stavrescu, Commander of the 14th Infantry Division; Colonel Constantin Lupu, Commander of the Garrison; Colonel Dumitru Captaru, county head; Constantin Chirilovici, who was in charge at the time; Gheorghe Leahu Police Superintendent; E. Giosanu and Matei Cosma, Police Inspectors; Gheorghe Stanciulescu, Secretary of the Central Police Station; Ion Aburel, Attorney-General; Colonel Gheorghe Barozzi, Military Judge of the 3rd Army; Major Nicolae Scriban, Military Judge of the 14th Division; Colonel Gheorghe Badescu, Superintendent of the Gendarmerie in Iasi; Captain Constantin Darie, Commander of the Police Squadron; Sub-Lieutenant Aurel Trindaf and Lance-Sergeant Forin Ghiveraru. Police officers and one or two Gendarmes units were also present. No one took any measures. General Stavrescu tried to stop the Romanian soldiers only when the massacring beasts became exhausted. Only then did he go to General von Salmuth, Commander of the 30th German Corps, whom he took with him to the Central Police Station, and who then ordered the few remaining Germans to leave. The Jewish survivors, however, were still in prison; among the guards there were both Romanians and Germans.

In the meantime, a lorry from the Town Hall started to collect the dead bodies lying in the streets.

18.00 hrs, June 29, 1941

There is almost complete silence in the town. The shooting has stopped, as has the howling, cheering and chanting of the mob. German loudspeakers have ceased bellowing out waltzes, instead, the speech of Major Nicolae Scriban, Military Judge of the 14th Infantry Division, is broadcast. He calls on soldiers to return to barracks, and for civilians to go home, but also orders that doors and windows should be kept open.

In the yard of the Central Police Station there are about 2,500 Jews left, the survivors. They are guarded by the Romanian authorities and a small number of German officers and soldiers. General Stavrescu orders their evacuation from the town and sends Police Superintendent Chirilovici to

Colonel Captaru (county head) with a message to ask permission from the Ministry of the Interior for his action. General Ion Popescu (Jack), Deputy State Secretary of the Ministry of the Interior, gives his consent to the order for evacuation. A document of the time, however, proves that the order was issued by Mihai Antonescu, Deputy President of the Council of Ministers, with a note that one group was to be evacuated to Targu Frumos, and the other to Podul Iloaei. Colonel Captaru also refers to a telephone conversation with Mihai Antonescu concerning the same issue.

Lieutenant-Colonel Chirilovici, however, in his report of September 15, 1941 to the Offices of the Gendarmerie in Iasi expresses doubt as to whether the Ministry of the Interior should play any role in the evacuation from Iasi of the Jews who were arrested on June 29. He claims that the order was issued by the 14th Division, which perhaps turned to the 3rd Army for the necessary freight cars. It seems the first version is the true one.

The evacuation was prepared with great haste. The first transportation of the first group was organized in the evening at 2000 hrs approx.; originally Romanian guards had been ordered to the scene but matters soon found their way into the hands of the German beasts, who encircled the marching column with two armored vehicles, and motorcyclists as well as a small number of officers and soldiers. There were also Romanian soldiers among the those providing the escort, but most were policemen, who added to the sufferings of the evacuees. Those who organized the evacuation did not do anything to mitigate the sufferings of the evacuees. Beatings, torture and robberies continued along the entire length of the journey to the station, but the most terrible incidents occurred in the square in front of the station and on the platform, while the evacuees were being loaded into the freight cars, and while Major Nicolae Scriban, Military Judge of the 14th Division, looked on.

Colonel Mavrichi, the representative of General Headquarters at the railway station in Iasi, placed 50 carriages at the disposal of Colonel Captaru - originally it had been presumed that approx. 2,500 Jews were to be transported. However, 12 carriages were withheld because they were cattle wagons equipped with air holes, and not ordinary freight cars, whose air holes could be sealed completely This fact is worthy of mention—since it is an indication of the calculated cruelty—and because in the end, it was of little significance, given the fact that fewer than 38 of the available carriages were used. The 2,430 people were forced to lie down on their stomachs in the square in front of the station, and threatened with instantaneous death should they lift their heads or dare to whisper; first they were robbed, then were counted under the light of the armored vehicles and motorcycles, and finally made to line up on the platform in single file, while soldiers pushed them into the carriages with bayonets and the butts of their rifles. The final carriages were not so crowded. Consequently, from among the lucky ones who got into these—even though they suffered greatly—there was only one death before the train reached Targu Frumos, an old man with a white beard. The number of people in each of the other carriages was approx. 150, almost four times higher than the intended capacity of the wagons. They suffered terribly, and the number of fatalities was incredibly high.

02.00 hrs, June 30, 1941

After the doors of the carriages had been locked and the ventilation holes sealed, the train carrying 2,430 Jews set off for Targu Frumos; policemen from Iasi, under the command of Lance-Sergeant Ion Leucea provided the escort. At approximately 07.00 hours the train passed through Targu Frumos; the railway officers and the local authorities did not order it to stop. They had been informed of the train's arrival by Colonel Captaru, county head, at approx. 11.00 hrs, on the previous night. Unsure as to whether or not the train would arrive, the local authorities, especially the Jewish Religious Community had somehow prepared themselves. Meanwhile, the evacuees were taken on a different route; first to Pascani, from there to Lespezi, then back to Pascani, and later in the direction of Roman, then back to Pascani again, until, finally, in the evening the train arrived in Targu Frumos. By that time the leading local authorities were under the impression that the train had been deliberately ordered to travel around in circles so as to lengthen the sufferings of its passengers, thus killing more people.

In Targu Frumos, Captain Marinescu Danubiu, Deputy Commander of the Garrison, with anger and hostility, received the train carrying the dead, the dying and those who could still be saved; he objected to unloading the freight cars, but when he realized that he was in no position to rebel against higher commands, turned to a German officer, and with his help the captain succeeded in depriving those who might still have been saved of their last chance. That night only 3 carriages were unloaded, and about 200 people transferred from them. They were continually beaten and tortured by German and Romanian soldiers and policemen (especially by Ion Botez, a police officer, who surpassed others in this activity). The prisoners were taken to the synagogue, where they begged for water in vain. Those who tried to give them water—the Leader of the Jewish Religious Community included—were beaten terribly in the presence of the Deputy Mayor, Dumitni Atudorei, who was busy looting at the time. That morning they were taken back to the station, and packed into carriages yet again. Those few who attempted to find water to drink were shot dead.

Meanwhile, the county head, Colonel Captaru, and the Ministry of the Interior—in the form of General Ion Popescu, its State Secretary—bowed to the demands of Captain Marinescu Danubiu, and halted the unloading of the carriages, and directed the train towards Calarasi-Ialomita.

The Office of the Gendarmerie in Iasi sent out 30 Gendarmes to Targu Frumos under the command of Sub-Lieutenant Aurel Triandaf and non-commissioned officer Anastase Bratu to act as guards for the new marching section. On Tuesday, July 1 at approx. 07.00 hrs they relieved Sub-Lieutenant Dan Chitescu, who, with 100 soldiers from the railway battalion, had guarded the Jews, preventing the able-bodied from escaping, and the dying from getting a drop of water. On a few occasions, however, their alertness was overcome: the evacuees managed to get a few buckets of water from the engine carriage; they had to pay 10,000 lei for each bucket.

Only in the morning were the dead bodies removed from the carriages by Gypsies tempted by the chance of looting them. This activity continued almost all day on Tuesday, July 1. Occasionally, however, they stopped for a while whenever an order came through on the telephone from Colonel Mavrichi, the representative of General Headquarters. He had just ordered the immediate departure of the train, when a miracle, which saved the lives of several people, occurred. A train was derailed at the Cuza Voda station, rendering the track unuseable for several hours. Meanwhile, almost all of the dead bodies could be taken out of the carriages. If not for this accident, the train would have departed with a large number of dead bodies, and this would undoubtedly have resulted in a higher number of deaths, and the increased suffering of the survivors.

The train stopped for approx. 24 hours in Targu Frumos, so that the bodies of dead Jews could be removed. During this time, this was the only act which eased the suffering of the others. With stubborn cruelty, however, it was forbidden to leave the doors open. This was done to prevent air from being let in. The evacuees were made to suffer accurately, and were denied water. At 1600 hours on July 1 the train left the station. The commander of the guards was Tribunal Judge, Aurel Triandaf.

The corpses removed in Targu Frumos were brought to the local Jewish cemetery, some on lorries, others pulled along the ground. The bodies, which were thrown onto lorries and into holes, had already started to decompose, hands, feet and pieces of flesh came apart from the trunks. Only after their clothes had been pulled off, were the 634 bodies buried in two holes 30 metres wide. The living were also among those thrown into the holes. Only one of the people pulled out managed to regain complete consciousness afterwards. Straw was thrown into one hole, and then either petrol or paraffin was poured on before it was set ablaze. The bodies burnt all night long.

06.00 hrs, June 30, 1941

With the same barbaric cruelty, another 1,902 Jews were taken to the station in Iasi. Several of them had been arrested the day before the pogrom. More had been locked up in the cellar of the Central Police Station. Others, survivors of the massacre in Alecsandri Alley that afternoon, were locked into the building of the Gendarme Legion. The rest were dragged out of their beds or hiding places on Sunday night or Monday morning, and taken to the Central Police Station, or directly to the railway station in specially ordered lorries. They were escorted by members of the Gendarmerie and police officers under the command of Police Officer C. Georgescu. German soldiers also joined them. The executioners treated them in exactly the same way they had treated the other group a few hours previously; they were robbed, counted and then forced to run - in single file - along the line of attackers as far as the freight cars. The station-master's office provided 30 carriages, but only 18 were used, into which the 1,902 Jews were packed. With 106 people in each carriage the intended capacity was exceeded three times. However, due to the disorderly manner in which the prisoners were loaded, there were fewer people in certain carriages, while others held as many as 150 crowded together. As a result, when death set in, the corpses remained upright among the dying and the living. The suffering of the people packed into the second train lasted for a shorter period, but was more appalling than that experienced by those transported before them. There were carriages in which a person died every two or three minutes, and those still alive longed for death as their redemption. By the time the journey had ended, in certain carriages there were only two or three survivors wasting away among more than 100 dead bodies. Before the train departed 80 corpses were put into the last carriage, these had been collected earlier at the station; some of them had been shot dead, others bayoneted, but most had been bludgeoned to death with the hammers the staff at the station used to test the wheels of trains. A period of eight hours had elapsed between the loading of the prisoners in Iasi and the time when the train stopped in Podul Iloaiei (20 kms away). This was sufficient time for 1,194 of the 1,902 people to die - the latter figure was actually 2,000. If they had walked, the journey would have been shorter, and nobody would have died.

When the survivors were ordered out of the freight cars at Podul Iloaiei station, they were met by Sergeant Ursache. By this time they had degenerated into imbecilic wrecks incapable of walking, eating, drinking, crying, cursing or hating. First they were taken to the synagogue, and later to the homes of local Jews; they lived there in misery for almost three months.

June 30, 1941

By Monday morning events were coming to an end in the yard of the Central Police Station in Iasi. The wailing of the last of the dying was the only sound to be heard from among the bodies piled on top of one another. An enormous pool of blood spread from the middle of the yard, on and on, as far as the gate; it saturated the shoes of all those who had to cross it. Beside the fence bodies were stacked in piles like logs.

Every employee from the firm of undertakers was mobilized to clean the area. Four tips, each capable of transporting 20-30 bodies, and 24 rubbish-carts, able to handle 10 bodies each, were used all day long to take the corpses to the Jewish cemetery and other places, the exact locations of which still remain unknown. One particular tip made eight return journeys. At the Jewish cemetery the bodies were thrown into a huge hole, which—coincidentally—had been dug ten days previously under the orders of the commanders of the civil defense. The bodies were thrown from the carts into the hole, and onto one another: the dead, the dying and the slightly injured. /..../

June 30, 1941

General Stavrescu washed his hands of the affair just as Pontius Pilate had done, and went out to the front-line during the night. He issued a decree in which he blamed the events of the nights of 28-29 on terrorists working for the enemy. He ordered a curfew and restricted the carrying of arms. Finally, he threatened to blow up houses and execute hostages. On the previous evening, Major Nicolae Scriban, Military Judge of the 14th Division, had had the decree announced over loud-speakers on automobiles.

July 1, 1941

Ion Antonescu makes an announcement, which is broadcast on radio and reported in the press at home and abroad. According to his report, 500 Jewish communists were shot dead in Iasi, after opening fire on German and Romanian soldiers from their houses.

July 1, 1941

Colonel Constantin Lupu, Commander of the Garrison, appointed Military Commander of the town on the night following the massacre, issues a decree. He proclaims that, from now on, the inhabitants of houses, from which shots are fired at German or Romanian soldiers, will be executed following a 'brief investigation'. This decree seemed wise, because the authorities knew that the snipers had been Germans or Iron Guard members, who had wanted to provoke the massacre. However, by the time the decree was posted, the citizens had already been completely brainwashed, and even the children of Iasi believed that the shots had been fired from Jewish houses. Therefore, the decree was considered a reinforcement of the rumors, and the atmosphere became even more threatening. Naturally, the decree did not contain any threats against those who continued to kill Jews. These murders were now only isolated incidents, mostly affecting the suburbs. The number of victims was not as high any more because the frightened Jews were in hiding, and did not dare walk in the streets.

July 2, 1941

Another announcement from Ion Antonescu declared that 50 Jewish communists from among the those 'alien to the nation' would be shot dead for each German or Romanian soldier killed.

July 2, 1941

The train under the command of Sub-Lieutenant Aurel Triandaf, which had departed from Targu Frumos the previous day, arrived in Mircesti at dawn. Here, 327 dead bodies were removed from the freight cars; they were buried on the edge of a village called Iugani. The doors of the carriages were left open only long enough to remove the bodies. No water was given to the people, who had gone crazy from thirst. They drank urine and sucked the blood and pus out of one another's wounds. Those who jumped out of the carriages either to escape or drink from the puddles of rainwater were shot dead.

July 3, 1941

The train arrived at the next station, in Sabaoani, and then continued to Roman, where it was not allowed into the station because of the stench emanating from it. Under the order from General Headquarters, which was located in the town, the train was redirected to Sabaoani, where about 300 corpses were removed. A medical committee also arrived on the scene, and ordered that water be given to the people. Only then, on the fifth day of their suffering, were the evacuees allowed to drink some water. Some of them, completely dehydrated, collapsed as if struck by lightning as the water was lifted to their lips.

July 6, 1941

The train continued its journey. In Roman, a further 55 bodies were removed, and some of the evacuees were washed. Their rags, however, were burnt, so they had to continue almost completely naked. The train was freed of 10 bodies in Marasesti, 40 in Inotesti, and finally it arrived in Calarasi. Here, Sub-Lieutenant Aurel Triandaf was not able to hand over more than 1,011 living, 69 dying and 25 dead persons from the 2,430 who had been loaded onto the train in Iasi, a figure which had decreased to 1,776 by the time he took over in Targu Frumos.

The survivors were accommodated in a warehouse in the yard of the barracks of the 23rd Infantry Regiment. Throughout the two months they spent in Calarasi, they lived in miserable conditions, despite being aided by the Union of Jewish Religious Communities, and the fact that the local authorities were relatively well-disposed towards them. Unsurprisingly, it was almost impossible to relieve their sufferings. They were in such a terrible state that of the 1,100 people there, 25 were buried on the first day, and from then on 6-7 died daily, and 95 had to be hospitalized; two thirds of them were completely naked and the rest were wearing nothing but their shirts. /..../

August 1941

Iasi is calm again. Conditions in the town could almost be described as normal. Due to the urges or threats of the authorities, the Jewish women of Iasi had to take the place of the men, whose bodies were rotting in huge common graves, or who were suffering in internment camps in Podul Iloaei and Calarasi.

The town is flooded with organizations conducting investigations: the Ministry of the Interior, General Headquarters, the Special Information Service, etc. Each has sent a representative to investigate the causes and circumstances of the pogrom, and the terrible crimes committed. Not one, however, dared find anyone guilty.

General Emanoil Leoveanu, Senior Director of the Siguaranta, sent by General Ion Antonescu himself, was only able to carry out superficial enquiries, because, about three hours after his arrival, the German military authorities asked him to leave town. However, his time spent there was enough for him to establish that no Jew had fired at the army, and that not one single German or Romanian soldier had been wounded, the entire chaotic event had been nothing other than an orchestrated Iron Guard or fascist charade, organized for the purpose of exterminating Jews.

Despite the fact that, through these investigations, every leading personality became acquainted with the truth, nobody thought that the lethal poison, with which the soul of the masses had been impregnated, should be neutralized.

The contrary was to be the case. Hardly had the frenzied atmosphere begun to normalize than the new military commander of the town, General Dumitru Carlaont, issued an edict that all Jews were to wear signs to distinguish themselves from other citizens. This served to create fresh conditions for anxiety and suffering. As a result of the same edict, a number of Jews from Iasi were chased out of their homes, and forbidden to take anything with them, apart from their clothes.

The avalanche of measures against Jews began: the organization of labor service, loan subscriptions, the expulsion of tenants and owners from their flats, deportation to Transnistria, etc.

These measures, however, were still not enough to satisfy some officials. New attempts were made at organized provocation; as in the case when 'provocative objects' were found in the synagogue in German Street, among the objects in question was a portrait of Stalin, which may have been planted there by the police.

As frame-ups and acts of provocation showed no signs of success, officials turned to the central authorities with their ghastly proposals. Police Superintendent Lieutenant-Colonel Constantin Chirilovici— mistakenly considered conscientious and well-disposed by many Jews —expressed his satisfaction to the government with what the army had done on June 29, but expressed his regret that little had been achieved during the pogrom.

Selected Documents

1.

Presidium of the Council of Ministers, Bucharest, Information Centre, June 19, 1941

Ref No.62783

Ministry of National Propaganda

Confidential

I hereby enclose the Information Memorandum concerning the activities of the Secret Service under the authority of the Ministry of National Propaganda, in which Mr. Antonescu, the Leader of the State, introduced the following resolutions:

The resolutions noted in the text are to be executed;

All the Jewish-communist coffee houses in Moldavia are to be shut down;

The names of all Jewish and communist agents or sympathizers are to be listed (by county).

The Ministry of the Interior is to restrict their freedom of movement, so as to ensure that the Ministry will be able to execute further orders to be given by me concerning them, when the suitable time comes.

The office, which collects the data—from Bessarabia and Bucovina—of the suffering of citizens, and of crimes committed under Bolshevik rule, should stand by for action, so that we can make use of this data immediately throughout the country, in factories, cinemas and in schools.

Apart from this, His Highness has approved all the proposals of the Ministry of National Propaganda, which were submitted to him under proposal No. 83/M on May 31, 1941, and which are also indicated in the enclosed memorandum.

You are requested to take action and report the results of measures taken by you to the Presidium of the Council of Ministers (Central Information Service) by July 10, 1941.

By order of the Presidium of the Council of Ministers General I. Steflea m.p.

***

2.

Presidium the Council of Ministers   July 1, 1941

Announcement

The Soviets are attempting to organize acts of sabotage, revolt and violence behind the front through all means at their disposal.

For this purpose they are deploying spies and terrorist agents from aeroplanes by parachute. These in turn contact agents operating in the country and within the Jewish-communist community for the purpose of jointly organizing violent actions.

A number of these agents have been arrested, and attempts at acts of violence have been avenged.

In Iasi 500 Jewish-communists, who had opened fire on German and Romanian soldiers were executed.

Every attempt at disrupting public order and peace, must be firmly avenged on sight.

It is the duty of peace-loving citizens to immediately report to the authorities any suspicious elements or aliens who have recently appeared in towns and villages. Those who fail to report elements seeking to threaten order and security in time, will be hanged along with their families. /..../

***

3.

Presidium of the Council of Ministers   July 2, 1941

Announcement

Recently there have been several cases of elements alien to our nation and against our interests opening fire on German and Romanian soldiers.

Each repetition of this ghastly violent act must be relentlessly avenged.

For each murdered German or Romanian soldier we will execute 50 Jewish-communists.

***

4.

Military Court of Justice

Examining Magistrate's Office No.1

Minutes

In reference to the interrogation of witness Eugen Cristescu, ex-Head of the Special Information Service (SSI).

I was Head of the Special Information Service when Marshal Antonescu was in power.

There was a total of 11 German information services in operation in Romania. (...) As I discovered during my investigation, three German secret service groups, operating under cover, were involved in the events in Iasi:

1. The Gestapo (...);

2. The Sicherheits Dienst (...);

3. The Geheime Feldpolizei (...);

/.../

The Investigation:

Upon discovering that official investigations had not thrown light on the plot which provoked the violent actions of the Germans in

Iasi, and since I was not satisfied with the information given me
by two of my officials, whom I had sent to Iasi on July 15, 1941 in
the aftermath of the massacre, I personally went to Iasi with the
detachment to conduct an investigation in the hope of discovering
how the massacre had been plotted. In June 1946. I found out
that the file on this examination had disappeared from the Archives of the Special Information Service. Consequently, I am at
present attempting to reconstruct events from memory, as far as
possible, and on this basis, I can state that the Germans instigated acts of provocation around the Central Police Station in
Iasi, and opened fire on soldiers of the Todt-corps, who had been
Stationed in Iasi in large numbers; none of these soldiers was injured, nevertheless, they began to slaughter the Jews.

Therefore, the so-called Jewish uprising at the Central Police
Station of Iasi was in actual an act of provocation, executed by
German and Romanian elements working for the German secret
services, which had operated under cover: the Gestapo, the SD
and the Geheimfeldpolizei.

The Abwehr had nothing to do with this case, because its agents
were in the first line at the front carrying out reconnaissance and
counter-intelligence missions.

During the investigation, it came to light that the Romanians had
been recruited from among the well-known anti-Semitic elements
in Iasi. These were agents of the above-mentioned German secret services; they were led by a certain Martinescu, and used
German weapons during the act of provocation.

The names of other Germans and Romanians involved in the
provocation in Iasi were also mentioned in the file.

I had intended to arrest culpable Romanians, but I discovered
that Germans had already helped them to flee to Germany. I also
suspected that Major Gregori and Captain Rochscheid were involved in the Iasi case. I ordered their expulsion from the country.

I reported all of these facts to ex-Marshal Antonescu, who made
a note of them so as to be able to discuss them with General
Schobert, Commander of the Southern Army. /...../

***

5

The testimony of Lieutenant-Colonel Trajan Borcescu, ex-Head of the Secretariat of the SSI, interrogated by Dumitru Saracu, public prosecutor, on November 12, 1945.

I was an employee of Department No.2 of General Headquarters, which dealt with military counter-intelligence, from 1938 to April 1, 1941.

On April 1,1941 I was transferred to the Special Information Service (SSI), where I presented myself on May 1, 1941. /..../

On November 11,1940, Eugen Cristescu, who had been Director of the, Ministry of the Interior until that date, became the Head of the Special Information Service. /..../

I saw a photographic record of the massacre in Iasi. It also contained explanatory notes next to the photographs. The collection was compiled by Director Florin Becescu-Georgescu, and Gheorghe Cristescu (the brother of Eugen Cristescu). The former wrote the explanatory notes, the latter took the pictures. This album was sent by courier from the detachment to Mihai Antonescu. In the explanatory notes they justified the pogrom in Iasi by claiming that Jews, aided by Soviet partisans, had opened fire on German and Romanian soldiers marching to the front. It was claimed that on this occasion approx. 20,000 Jews were killed in Iasi, mostly in the districts of Pacurari and Sararie, in Lapusneanu Street, at the Central Police Station, and at other places.

According to them, the massacre was organized by German SS-members, policemen, and Romanian soldiers.

It is my suspicion that the preparation and planning for the Iasi massacre was the work of the 1st Mobile Detachment, because Eugen Cristescu said to me upon returning to Bucharest: "All the great things we did in Moldavia were carried out in co-operation with Department No.2 of Headquarters: with Colonel Dinulescu and Lieutenant-Colonel Petrescu Gheorghe".

Grigore Petrovici told me that Junius Lecca had played a significant role in the preparation of the pogrom. He was the Head of the Counter-Intelligence Residency at the centre in Iasi, and supplied information concerning Jewish hot-beds of activity in Iasi; this information was handed over to Eugen Cristescu, who formulated the plans for the Iasi massacre, along with Department No.2 of General Headquarters and the German Commander.

At the end of the explanatory notes in the album, which I have already mentioned, it was written that the detachment, following an agreement with Department No.2 of General Headquarters had taken action on the issue of evacuating the Jewish survivors from Iasi.

The photographs in the album showed a number of houses in Iasi. Bullet-holes could be seen in the walls; it was claimed that these impressions were the result of bullets fired by Jews at German and Romanian soldiers. Apart from these, there were two more photos, in which Romanian and German soldiers could be seen lying in the street. In the explanatory notes it was claimed that they had been killed by Jews.

The other photographs showed streets in the Jewish districts full of the corpses of the victims of the pogrom.

Concerning the preparation of the Iasi massacre, I must add that the Directors of the Iasi Information Centre of the Special Information Service, Captain Balotescu Gheorghe and Major Tulbure, were the ones who recruited Iron Guards, and both of them took part in the preparation and organization of the massacre with the Mobile Detachment of the SSI.

Concerning the executions, although the detachment was not commissioned for this purpose, the following units, consisting of members of the detachment, took part in the massacre: a squad headed by Captains Grigore Petrovici and Gheorghe Balotescu, another under the leadership of Major Tulbure, and a third directed by Gheorghe Cristescu-Gica, the brother of Eugen Cristescu. I am only aware of these squads, but there may have been others as well. The units were under the control of Director Florin Becescu-Georgescu.

During the first days, the courier who had brought the photographic album informed me of the part played in the executions by these SSI units. Later, however, members of these groups themselves talked to me about it; to be more exact, Grigore Petrovici-Guta, Cristescu-Gica, Balotescu and my ex-secretary, Silvestru Radu P. Vernescu. They said that they had taken an active part in the execution of Jews throughout the pogrom. My ex-secretary, Silvestru Radu P. Vernescu, told me that he, along with Ionel Stanescu and Eugen Cristescu, had spoken to Marshal

Antonescu a few days before the pogrom. I suspect that, on that occasion, they discussed and arranged the pogrom.

Part of the hidden agenda of this Mobile Detachment was to either evacuate or deport the Jews from Moldavia, and for this purpose Florin Becescu-Georgescu, Director of the SSI, took the files of Jews and communists with him when he left for Bucharest.

The detachment traveled from Iasi to Kishinev, where they organized another bloodbath; in Kishinev the same SSI units operated. I also know that one member of the Service was caught robbing in Kishinev, and subsequently relieved of his post.

The detachment looted in Tighina and Tiraspol, and was involved in the massacre in Odessa. From Tighina onwards the detachment was led by Colonel Ion Lisievici, with Lieutenant-Colonel Vasile Palius as his deputy.

A part of the detachment, under the leadership of Major Olteanu, who was later succeeded by Major Tomescu Niculai, was accommodated in Cetatea Alba, where they looted the homes of Jewish citizens.

The other parts of the detachment, headed by Colonel Lisievici operated in Transnistria, the Ukraine and in the Krim Peninsula, and reached as far as Rostow; among them were Lieutenant-Colonel Vasile Palius, Director Trohani Nicolae, under the pseudonym Major Carlan, Lieutenant-Colonel Ernescu Grigore, Captain Rusu Victor, Captain Velicu Dudu, Lieutenant Mosoarca (reserve officer), Lieutenant Florin Begnescu, Racu, Deputy Director and many more.

The file of the Odessa cases was given to me personally by Grigore Petrovici, and that of the massacre in Kishinev by Gheorghe Cristescu-Gica. /.../

Public Prosecutor   Lieutenant-Colonel

D. Saracu m.p.   Trajan Borcescu m.p.

***

6.

The testimony of Lieutenant-Colonel M. Radulescu, interrogated by Divisional General Nedelea Savu, Special Investigating Magistrate, on June 12, 1947:

I can say very little about the massacre in Iasi because I was not there. But I think its political consequences were far too significant for it not to be taken into consideration, therefore I have tried to form a clear picture of its origins and progress.

The first thing which made it clearer to me was part of a conversation between Lieutenant-Colonel Constantin Ionescu Micandru and German Captain Alexandru von Stranschi, which I accidentally overheard. On St. Eugen's day (December 24, 1941), we celebrated the name day of the SSI Head Eugen Cristescu; during the banquet I sat next to Captain Stranschi, and at the end of the conversation I heard Lieutenant-Colonel Ionescu Micandru say about Jews:

"Don't worry, we will settle the Jewish issue just as we did in Iasi with the SSI; when some got fired, others took their place. Isn't that right, Sandu?" (Sandu was Captain Stranschi)

Divisional General Savu Nedelea,   Constantin Radulescu,

Special Investigating Magistrate   Lieutenant-Colonel

***

7.

From the testimony of witness Lieutenant-Colonel Traian Borcescu, interrogated by Dumitru Saracu, public prosecutor, on January 15 and 18, 1946.

I completely stand by my statement of November 12, 1945, which I wish to corroborate today.

I must add that it came to my mind that following the bloody incidents in Iasi, the couriers', who brought the post to the First Mobile Detachment of the SSI, told me that a group from the detachment, led by Deputy Police Commissar Grigore Petrovici, had been dispatched, and actively participated in events in the town. Grigore Petrovici had everyone call him "Inspector", even though he only held the rank of deputy police commissar. /.../

I know that Grigore Guta Petrovici, a member of the 1st Mobile Detachment, worked together with Major Gheorghe Balotescu in Iasi during the time of the pogrom. Petrovici and Balotescu themselves claimed that they had closely cooperated in executing orders received in Iasi and Kishinev.

I definitely know that Colonel Ioan Lissievici, who first became Deputy Commander, and then Commander of the First Mobile Detachment of the SSI, directly commanded all the spies and counter-intelligence officers, in other words, everyone operating at the front or behind it. That is how I know that the leaders of the Iasi Residency, Gheorghe Balotescu and Major Emil Tulbure, as well as members of their unit, were directly answerable to Colonel Ioan Lissievici. I know for sure that these two officers took part in the Iasi pogrom with their units, which were assembled from Iron Guard elements; Major Gh. Balotescu told me this. These two officers and their Iron Guard units laid the ground work for the pogrom, worked out the details of its plan, and then directly participated in the pogrom, together with other soldiers and civilians in Iasi.l

D. Saracu   Traian Borcescu

Public Persecutor m.p.   Lieutenant-Colonel m.p.

***

8.

Minutes of the Confrontation

July 7, 1945, 17.00 hrs

General Leoveanu Emanoil stated the following: On June 29, 1941, the then Minister of the Interior summoned me, and told me that the Iasi police had committed serious crimes. They had looted and organized a pogrom against the Jewish citizens; he stated that General Antonescu had ordered me to leave for Iasi immediately, and find out who was responsible. I immediately traveled to Iasi. I arrived on July 1, 1941, and set to work at once.

Based on what I experienced, I came to the conclusion that the Germans had provoked the affair, and the army made it look as if there had been shooting. This is borne out by the fact that bullets from Flaubert cap-pistols were found in the street. They only have a range of 3-4 metres. Besides, there was not one dead or wounded soldier in the streets.

I must add that during the days of the massacre the Jewish citizens were collected from their homes by the police, and escorted to the Central Police Station with the help of the garrison troops led by their commanders. During my investigation, I was able to conclude that Iron Guards cooperated with the police and soldiers of the town during the pogrom.

I then contacted Colonel Chirilovici, Police Superintendent, who reported that he had used all the means at his disposal to guarantee public order.

During conversations with Colonel Chirilovici, one of the things he told me was that once the shooting had started, the soldiers received an order to search houses to find out where the shots were coming from.

Citizens were chased out of their houses and arrested. A number of them were shot there and then, while more were taken to the Central Police Station, where they were abused; others were killed by the Germans.

I do not remember clearly whether or not Colonel Chirilovici reported that those collected from the yard of the Central Police Station had been shot there with machine guns; but I do recall him mentioning that they had been beaten up terribly.

I must add that in my report, I did not claim that police forces were also among the killers and robbers.

***

9.

From the testimony of Avram Hahamu, Deputy President of the Jewish Religious Community of Iasi, interrogated by Mihail Popilian, public prosecutor, on March 2, 1945.

I have been Deputy President of the Jewish Religious Community
of Iasi since 1938. On June 26, 1941, the Soviet Air Force
bombed Iasi. On June 27,1941, Colonel Chirilovici, Police Superintendent summoned the 12 leaders of the Community, including
myself, to the Central Police Station and in the name of the then
commanding general - I have forgotten his name, but I think he
was called Stavrescu - he stated that he had information that the
pilots of the Soviet planes were from Iasi, and we, Jews, had
given them signals, because this is the only explanation for the
demolition of the town and for the fact that no Jews were among
the victims, and neither did we suffer material losses. We immediately told him that we were not co-operating with the enemy,
and asked for twenty-four hours so that we could carry out our
own investigations.

The next day we submitted a report, in which the late Av.
Gherner indicated that in districts on the outskirts of the town,
where poor Jews lived, so far 38 Jews were dead and 100 Jewish houses collapsed due to the bombings; therefore the statement that we were in connection with the enemy could not be
held up and that we could not be held responsible for it.

The Police Superintendent said that he would report this to the
commanding general and at the same time ordered us to collect
all telescopes, torches, cameras and film-cameras within 48 hour,
and hand them in at the Central Police Station.

Popilian   Avram Hahamu m.p.

Public Prosecutor m.p.

****

10.

Testimony of Wolf Herscu, interrogated by Gh. Trissonimo, public
prosecutor of the Court of Appeal of Bucharest, on January 2,
1948.

When Iasi was bombed on June 26, 1941, I was injured in my leg
and neck. On that day, as far as I remember, a sergeant from either the Education or Training Department of the 13th Guardsmen Regiment came for me, but perhaps, he may have been
assigned to the Transport Corps. At the same time they also
came after Cojocaru Iosub and Leon Schechter. All three of us

were taken to the Romanian Headquarters in Vasile Lupu Street, from there we were escorted by armed guards to Division Headquarters in to Copou, and to the exhibition hall. I was escorted by the same Lance-Sergeant who had come for me. When we arrived, we were handed over to two captains, who, upon realizing our innocence, told us that we were free to go and ordered that we be escorted home. We left for home with the same escort, but then the Lance-Sergeant told us to take a different route, and directed us down a remote road, the Sararie lane, and from there towards the rifle range. Since I was barely able to walk, because of my injury from the bombardment, I had to lean on Cojocaru Iosub. Suddenly, I heard a bullet whistling past my head. That one only skimmed me, another, however, went straight into my left hip. While collapsing I saw that it was the Lance-Sergeant who had shot me, and it was also him who ordered me not to look back. I regained consciousness at dawn June 27, 1941.1 wanted to stand up, but I could not, and I saw that Cojocaru Iosub was lying dead in front of me about 10-12 metres away. He had been shot by the same Lance-Sergeant. While I was falling to the ground, I could hear him shouting at the other two to stay where they were.

Gh. Trissonimo m.p.   Wolf
Herscu m.p.

Public Prosecutor

***

11.

From: Regional Police Inspectorate, Iasi

To: Central Police Headquarters

  23621/June 29, 1941

This is a continuation of report No.23469 of June 29, 1941:

On June 18, at 10.00 hrs, a small number of independent army units in the district of Tatarasi began searching Jews, and while doing so abused them considerably, and committed serious offences against them.

As the local Chief of Police attempted to intervene, Lance-Sergeant Manoliu Mircea turned to a passing German corps and said that the local Jews had radio transmission equipment but he had been unable to find it because the police were protecting the Jews. The leader of the German corps offered to collaborate with the police during the rest of the house-searches. They were also joined by Romanian soldiers from the 13th Infantry Regiment and the 22nd Artillery Regiment. All of them continued to abuse the Jews.

When the commander of the garrison, Colonel Lupu, was informed of what was happening, Colonel Captaru, county head, the Military Judge of the Division along with the commanders of the aforementioned troops as well as representatives of the Central Police Station went to the scene and arrested the rebellious Lance-Sergeant and those (among the Romanians) who had actively taken part in the offences; they were handed over to the military judge of the division for investigation.

This action fully re-established peace in the district. On the same day at 22.00 hrs. the police force was informed that military units of vital importance were being shot at.

All local military bodies were informed immediately, first of all General Stavrescu, Commander of the Division. The Commander of the Garrison and the Military Judge went to the Central Police Station to study the situation and report to the Commander of the Division.

Patrols, consisting of Gendarme members and policemen, which were sent out during the day time, were immediately strengthened.

The conclusion: incidents of shooting were becoming more widespread in several districts of town, and in areas where German or Romanian soldiers were marching.

Consequently, a group of soldiers marching down Lascar Catargiu Street came under fire, as did another group marching through Carol Street. Even though the shooting was very heavy, nobody was injured. All night long the army, the police and the Germans searched the places from which shots were fired. No Jews were arrested for shooting. The Gendarme inspector sent two Christians to the Inspectorate. One of them, a certain Lupsanschi, claimed to be an Iron Guard. They found his will on him, which he had prepared the previous day. Weapons were not found on them.

Under orders from the Commander of the Division, at dawn the search of Jewish houses was started, but not one single weapon was found.

So far, approx. 2,500 Jews have been taken to the Central Police Station, the Commander of the Division wants to evacuate all of them from the town.

Not long ago, the police organizations informed me that certain Romanian and German soldiers were committing acts of abuses, and looting, and that many Jews have been killed in the streets, and even at the Central Police Station. /..../

E. Giosanu m.p. Regional Inspector

***

12.

From the testimony of Lieutenant-Colonel Romulus Muresanu, interrogated by General Emanoil Ionescu , specially appointed examining judge, on June 27, 1947.

In 1941, as a captain, I was deputy head of the Economics Office. As far as I know, on June 26, 1941, the Russians bombed Iasi, and in one of the planes there was a Jew from Iasi called Lupu, and another Jew; these were caught, and the German commander ordered the evacuation of Jews from the town. (...) On June 27, 1941, in the evening I was walking down Carol Street with my wife when someone fired at me. Shots were fired in Buna Vestire Street as well, but nobody was hit. A German patrol approached me, and asked where the shots had come from, and I indicated the direction. While I continued my walk I heard a round of machine-gun fire; later I learned that the Germans had executed the Jews in one of the houses. /.../

On June 28, I met Captain Capatana's orderly on Spiridonie Square; he was shooting at Jews. When I asked him who had given the order for this, he showed his surprise at my question, and asked: do you not know that there is an order to shoot every Jew? /... /

The officers of the 6th Rifle Regiment Stationed in Balti asked
the German Headquarters to which they were attached (as I have
been informed), to be sent to the front-line next to Sculeni (their
request was fulfilled), because the Jews there severely humiliated them when they had had to withdraw from Bessarabia, and
now they wanted to take their revenge. They did the same in
Balti, where I saw members of the 6th Rifle Regiment shoot Jews
dead. I heard in the officers' mess that Sub-Lieutenant Mihailescu
himself shot dead the Jews from Gura Cainari. As far as I know,
approx. 1,040 Jews were shot dead. /.../

General Ionescu m.p.   M. Muresan m.p.

specially appointed exam. judge   Lieut.-Col. res.

***

13.

6th Mountain Rifle Regiment
9801/July 31, 1941 Military Post Office No.10.
    To the General Command of the 14th Division

 To the adjutant's office

Reply to your order No.66 of July 30, 1941.

I hereby report that the regiment has already replied, by referring
to this issue in report No.700 of July 28, 1941.

In my opinion the methods employed by the regiment, while in
compliance with higher orders, were too tame, since the Jews
had dared to shoot at the Romanian army, and had dared to
carry out sabotage actions against it, which resulted in the loss of
many soldiers who could have been saved.

Captain Stihi executed those bastards. They do not bear thinking
about; this occurred as the result of an order given by me, and in
full compliance with higher commands in relation to issues of this
type.

I enclose a copy of the above-mentioned report.

Commander of the 6th Mountain Rifle Regiment:

Colonel Maties Ermil m.p.

***

14.

From the testimony of Colonel Mihai Isacescu, interrogated by General Emanoil Ionescu , specially appointed examining judge, on June 18, 1947.

At the time of the Bessarabian military expedition I was the commander of the reconnaissance squadron of the 6th Rifle Regiment, as its captain. (...) When we captured the Sculeni-Rusi bridge-head, I heard that in Stanca Rosnoveanu, Captain Stihi, Sub-Lieutenant Mihailescu and private Ion Epure had killed the Jews who had escaped from Sculeni-Rusi, and that private Epure had mutilated them prior to execution. /..../

I was informed by word of mouth by fellow-soldiers, Captain Ioachim and others, that the above-mentioned people had done this primarily to rob the Jews of the gold they had on them. The spoils were probably shared with Captain Stihi and Colonel Maties. In reference to this, a conversation about a watch between Captain Stihi's wife and Colonel Maties comes to mind. /.../

It is not true that in Marculesti the citizens first put up the white flag and then attacked Captain Otel's squadron by joining the Russian troops. The truth is that a Russian unit, approx. the size of a squadron, attacked Captain Otel's squadron from the side causing the soldiers to retreat, then the Russians withdrew and took with them Captain Otel, who was wounded in the leg. A story was subsequently concocted to cover up the stupidity of a squadron being dispatched, with neither backup nor reconnaissance units, towards the North-Eastern Heights of Floresti on the Vesdova-Alexen line, where they would have had to construct battle trenches before the arrival of the regiment.

General Ionescu Emanoil m.p

Colonel M. Isacescu,specially appointed examining judge m.p.

***

15.

From the testimony of Lieutenant Andronic Prepelita, a former
sergeant in Captain Stihi's squadron, interrogated by Captain Ion
Zaharescu , military examining judge, on May 7, 1947. /.../

It was Captain Stihi who carried out the execution of the Jews in
Stanca Rosnoveanu together with Sub-Lieutenant Mihailescu and
Sergeant Vasile Mihailov .

I must add that the machine-gun was operated by Sergeant
Vasile Mihailov. Captain Stihi and Sub-Lieutenant Mihailescu,
however, were equipped with one machine pistol each. They
made Jews stand in front of them in three columns, each with a
selection of men, women and children. The above-mentioned
three persons shot at them.

Captain Ion Zaharescu m.p   Prepelita Andronic

military examining judge   Lieutenant m.p.

***

16.

The Report of the Judicial Medical Examiner

The undersigned, Dr. Vasile Hurghisiu, the medical examiner of
the Jasi Judiciary, on the basis of official document No. 15152,
dated September 12, issued by the Chief Prosecutor of the Iasi
Judiciary, as well as the decisions made in response to petitions
Nos. 2171 and 2176 by the Iasi Jewish Religious Community,
dated September 10, 1945 and September 12, 1945, and with
reference to my oath, was invited "to take part in the exhumation
of Jewish remains buried in mass graves in Stanca Rosnoveanu
in order to verify the existence of the corpses in the mass graves,
and ascertain other relevant circumstances, for the purposes of
launching a criminal investigation or using the report as evidence
in criminal investigations in their enquiry or sentencing periods."

Historically: the above-mentioned two letters by the Iasi Jewish
Religious Community, addressed to the Office for Public Prose-
cutions of the Iasi Courts, indicate that on June 27, 1941 in
Stanca Rosnoveanu in Iasi county Jews were murdered and buried in mass graves.

It turns out from the testimony given by a witness, forty-year -old agricultural laborer, Zaharia Alexandru, from the village of Carpiti, that on a working day in 1941, a great number of Jews were brought to the above-mentioned site, where they were executed with machine guns set up approx. twenty metres from the victims and the hole, and fired by a captain and the soldiers of the 6th Rifle Regiment Stationed in Balti. The witness also states that he knows of and can identify four mass graves, and knows of one further grave but is unable to locate it, because it was dug beside a road which was subsequently rerouted.

The topographical description of the graves in Stanca Rosnoveanu: the corpses of Stanca Rosnoveanu, referred to in the report, were exhumed from three mass graves; the graves were at the foot of a hill in a valley approx. 12 kms from Iasi, near the village of Carpiti. They were located almost in a line next to one another, with a distance of only 2-3 meters between graves.

The sizes of the graves: Length: 6 ms;   Width: 3.5-4 ms
Depth: 1.5-1.7 ms

The exhumation began at the grave the farthest from Iasi (the closest to Carpiti), hereinafter referred to as No.I, the grave in the middle as No.II, and the third, (the closest to Iasi as No.III. The latter narrows towards the end.

Preliminary remarks:

The exhumation work began at grave No.I on September 12, 1945, and continued at grave No.II, and then at No.III. The work was periodically halted on public holidays and because of inclement weather. Due to the above circumstances, as well as the season, during that autumn, the Iasi Jewish Religious Community agreed to postpone the continuation of work on the exhumation. The exhumed bodies were buried in three large common graves in the Jewish cemetery. The digging was done by German POWs guarded by Soviet soldiers.

The description of the corpses:

Position: after the removal of a 30-50 cm layer of earth, the first layer of corpses appears. It can be established, that in all three graves, the bodies were positioned in a certain order. The heads are on either side of the hole. The bodies and limbs are entwined, making exhumation difficult and lengthy. In grave No.III, we found small children, their arms embracing the necks of female corpses. Most of the women had covered their faces with their head-scarfs or hands.

Clothing: The corpses were wearing "civilian" clothes characteristic of this province. The types of clothing varied differently. On some corpses there were two or three shirts, coals or overcoats, on others, especially the women in grave II, there were only nightdresses; the men in grave III were lying barefoot, scantily dressed or with rolled-up sleeves. We found the usual personal belongings in the pockets: keys, combs, handkerchiefs, stockings, bottles for water and perfume, etc. We also found jewelry on some corpses. We catalogued these, and attached the list to the examiner's report.

We carried out the identification of the corpses, to determine whether the male bodies had been circumcised—a traditional Jewish custom—(unless the process of rotting had not advanced too far). We also found various documents, issued to Jewish names. In this way, in one of the pockets of a male corpse we found a Soviet passport and a soldier's book, issued to the name Itic Motolevici, born in 1910 in Sculeni. We also found a birth certificate issued to the name Ghetel from Sculeni, as well as an identity card issued in Sculeni, which belonged to Faibis, born on June 13, 1907. The examination and identification of the clothes and documents was carried out by Dr. Germanski in the presence of Mr. Josef Michel, the representative of the Iasi Jewish Religious Community, during the reburial at the Iasi Jewish Cemetery.

Sex and age: the identification of the sex of the corpses was carried out on bodies less affected by rotting, by examining genitalia and bone structure. We also drew information from the clothes and documents. As far as age is concerned, in lack of other criteria, the identification was carried out on the basis of the Judicial Medical Examination, taking into consideration milk-teeth and the set of teeth characteristic of adults.

The number of bodies exhumed from the three mass graves was 311 (three hundred and eleven). In grave No.I 95, in grave No.II, 119, and in grave No.III, 97 corpses were found. /..../

Conclusions:
1. In the three mass graves from Stanca Rosnoveanu in Iasi county described in this report, 311 corpses of both sexes and all ages were found.

2. The documents found on the bodies, and the circumcision characteristic of Jews, prove that the bodies were of Jewish origin.

3. In the course of the judicial medical examination, we found that on most bodies, the multiple injuries caused by bullets are in the mid part of the bodies (the breast and the abdomen), and less frequently in the head.

4. In the case of some bodies, fracture of the skull can also be observed in addition to injuries caused by bullets. No injury whatsoever was found in the bone structure of a young child (2-4 yrs) after his skeleton was completely reassembled.

5. In mass grave No. I, which we dug out on the basis of witnesses' reports, the number of middle-aged men is higher; in grave No.II mostly the corpses of women and old people were found; there was a great number of children, women and old people in grave No.III; and only the corpses of six middle-aged men.

6. The clothing on the corpses is generally scanty. Many women were wearing night dresses or gowns, the men and children are barefoot.

Judicial Medical Examiner of Iasi:

Dr. V. Hurghisiu m.p.

Commander of The Office of the Gendarmerie in Hubolca:

Sergeant-Major Petru Ghimes m.p.

Representatives of the Jewish Religious Community of Iasi:

Josef Froimovici m.p.

Aron Aronovici m.p.

Aron Froimovici m.p.

David Leizer m.p.

Iosef Michel m.p.

***

17

Iasi Central Police Station   Registered on
July 2

Ref. No.99, June 30,1941 under No.23857; file No.569/941.

To the Inspectorates of the Police and Siguranta   /..../

On 28th at 22.00 hrs, our organizations informed us that in certain districts automatic weapon fire was coming from every house. /.../

All the soldiers marching through these districts and every Gendarme patrol which had been dispatched during the day to every district of the town, as well as a number of off-duty police officers, started to search the houses from which, according to them, shots had been fired. Every Jew was taken away; most were found in the air-raid shelters.

On this occasion many of them were shot dead, and many were robbed. /.../

The chaos grew greater every second, and since the shootings had taken place in the vicinity of several important institutions, there were suspicions that someone wanted to occupy them; therefore we strengthened the guards around the central telephone exchange, the Central Police Station and the railway Station: in spite of these measures, we were unable to capture any of the marksmen.

I must add that there were no fatalities, and only one policemen was slightly hurt.

When the sun came up, a Romanian army corps, which had been marching along Lascar Catargiu Street, came under fire, as did another marching along Carol Street. /... /

There can be no doubt that an anti-Semitic atmosphere quickly established itself. This led to Jews being pulled out of air-raid shelters, houses and shops. They were taken without pretext to the Central Police Station. On 29th at 09.00 hrs there were already 1,800 persons there, women, children and men of all ages.

The hostile atmosphere fueled abuse and looting, especially when German soldiers killed a woman in broad daylight in a pub-

lic street. Afterwards, disgusted they threw the body into a pas-
sage-way.

Civilians from the low stratum of society also joined in.

From this moment on, the banishment of Jews was combined
with ghastly looting and beatings. All the different groups within
the army and even policemen were involved in these actions.
Scenes were photographed by the Germans, naturally the
scenes in which no German soldiers played a part.

The situation was alarming. The soldiers did not listen to anybody's commands any more. They were roamed freely around
the town; looting, beating, torturing and even murdering. /.../

Lieutenant-Colonel   Gh. Stanciulescu. m.p.

Chirilovici m.p.   Secretary of Central Police Station

Police Superintendent of Iasi

***

18.

Report of Lieutenant-Colonel C. Chirilovici, Police Superintendent
in charge,

Report on the Pogrom in Iasi.

Iasi Central Police Station   Confidential

Ref. No.99. June 30, 1941

Dear Minister,

/.../

On the morning of June 28 of this year, the commander of the
German advance party, which was marching through Tatarasi
district, was informed that the Jews living in that area had radio
transmission devices, with which they gave signals to enemy aircraft whenever a plane appeared over the town.

The Germans began to search the district thoroughly. The soldiers of the 13th Guardsmen Regiment, who were accommodated in the district, and those of the 24th Artillery Regiment also participated in the operation. They were led by a Lance-Sergeant of the 13th Guardsmen Regiment.

On this occasion, due to the provocative behavior of the Jews, the soldiers, and to a greater extent the Christian community who joined them, attacked the Jews and committed certain offences.

On the evening of June 28, at approx. 20.30 hrs, I was informed by the district police offices that all over town there was random gunfire from houses inhabited by Jews.

We were informed of the same fact by the German Headquarters also, while they were putting more patrols into action in the town. /... /

The aggressors had increased their fire power, and the patrols and units marching through the town returned fire. /.../

At this time (3 o'clock) special units consisting of Gendarmes, soldiers and policemen were formed, which proceeded to surround the buildings from which the shots were coming. They also checked every person found in the buildings. /...../

An atmosphere of hostility against Jews emerged, and as a consequence all the Jews were collected from the buildings from where the shots came, and taken to the Central Police Station.

Some Jews, who were aggressive and resisted, were abused, and those who turned out to be guilty beyond doubt were shot dead.

On the morning of June 29, at 09.00 hrs, there were approx. 1,000 Jews in the yard of the Central Police Station.   /.../

The Romanian citizens fully convinced that the communist Jews were shooting, attacked the Central Police Station denouncing every Jew living in a building from which shots were fired. /..../

On June 29, at approx. 13.15 hrs, shots were fired at German soldiers positioned around and in the yard of the Central Police Station. They became terribly angry that communists with their shooting had wanted to help the Jews escape. They, therefore, shot into the Jews, killing a number of them. /.../

Lieutenant-Colonel C.D.Chirilovici m.p.,

 Police Superintendent in Charge

***

19.

Secret   July 7, 1941 No.4457

Gendarme Central Station,   Gendarme Office Iasi

Gendarme Station   3rd Police Department

Secret recording No.33716

July 9, 1941

To Gendarme Central Station, Gendarme Office

In accordance with the telephone information received on June 30, 1941.

I hereby report, that the following facts have been established on the basis of the information I collected:

On July 30 two trains full of Jews left Iasi:

a/ The first contained 2,500 Jews;

b/ The second 1,900.

In the first train 1,194 Jews died during the journey.

The train was made stop at Podul Iloaei (Iasi), where the dead were buried, and the survivors accommodated by local Jews.

In the second train 650 Jews died between Iasi and Targu Frumos. They were buried in Targu Frumos; 327 died between Targu Frumos and Mircesti, they were buried in Mircesti.

Colonel Gh. Badescu m.p.,

Iasi Cendarme Superintendent

Lieutenant-Colonel Al. Manoil m.p.,

Head of Police Department and Headquarters

***

20.

Testimony of Viad Marievici, former Director of the Burial Service Company of Iasi's Mayor's Office, interrogated by Dumitru Saracu, public prosecutor, on July 21, 1945.

(...) at approx. 11.00 hrs, a Lance-Sergeant came to my office, and requested a closed transport vehicle. I gave him the van, and when he returned at about 14.00 hrs, the driver told me that they had transported Jewish bodies from the yard of the Central Police Station to the Jewish cemetery. (...) On June 30, 1941, I came into my office as usual, and immediately received the order from the police to present myself with all available means of transport (cars and carts) at the Central Police Station. I immediately did so, and asked Police Constable Iancu to order out Gendarmes and policemen to escort every car and cart. This happened after an argument between us, because I objected to his proposal that the bodies be collected only by workers of the burial service company. I did so to prevent the possible looting. I also asked Police Constable Iancu about the dying and wounded. After contacting Colonel Lupu, Commander of the Town, Police Constable Iancu told me that the dying and wounded should be taken to the Jewish hospital. I learnt from the staff of the burial company that this order had not actually been carried out, and in many cases dying people were also put onto the cars, as ordered by the Gendarme sergeants escorting the transporters These either suffocated as a result of being covered by dead bodies, or were thrown into the holes alive. I must add that only the staff carrying out physical work remained next to the cars and carts, and these orders were given only by soldiers and policemen. I supplied them with four vans and 24 carts then (...). The cartsmen always had lunch at the town eatery, but that day most of them did not appear there. In the evening they explained that the authorities held them back so as to continue transporting. A lot of them were drunk. I am convinced that most of them robbed the dead bodies, and this supposition can be proven by the fact that a few days later, when they received their wages, they did not even bother to count the money, and behaved as if they couldn't care less. A number of

them were wearing excellent quality clothes, which they could not
have afforded on their salaries.

In reference to the question of whether I consider the number 254
to be the precise number of dead bodies buried in the Jewish
cemetery, I must say - and I base my statement on the announcement issued at the time, which mentioned 500 Jewish
communists, and on what I saw in the yard of the police Station
and in Alecsandri Alley—the number of dead bodies exceeded
500. (...) On Monday morning I was refused entry to the yard of
the police Station. When the gate was opened, I saw a pile of
corpses, they were piled on top of one another like logs. There
was not enough room to drive a car into the yard. Blood ran down
as far as the gate, and when I entered, it completely covered my
shoes. - I must also add that I also saw the fence (...),and because there was an enormous number of corpses there, I asked
a policeman standing by it, who spoke with Bessarabian accent,
how come there were so many bodies. He replied: we brought a
lot of them here, too, to this place, and shot them dead.   /.../

D. Saracu public prosecutor m.p.   Vlad Marievici m.p.

***

21.

Romania. Ministry of Interior.   Secret

Iasi Central Police Station.   Confidential

135 CS/ August 23, 1941.

To the Office of the Highest Military Tribunal

We hereby transfer the enclosed report of August 1941 concerning the atmosphere of the citizens in the sphere of authority of the
Central Police Station.

Lieutenant-Colonel

Chirilovici m.p.   Anghel Z. Anghel m.p.

Police Superintendent of Iasi   Leader of Siguaranta

/.../

The mood and disposition of the citizens:

At the beginning of the military operations against the Soviet
forces, the Romanian citizens welcomed the war with enormous
energy and enthusiasm. We are fighting for the liberation of the
occupied territories and especially for the destruction of
Bolshevism. (...) At the time of the disturbances of the current
year, June 29-30, the Romanian citizens showed a implacable
hatred towards Jews, as they considered them exponents of the
internal communist powers, which are attempting to destroy the
country and the defeat the allied forces. They also accused the
Jews of being the only minority to hide and protect Soviet parachutists and terrorists. When measures were taken by the army
against Jews, the Romanian citizens unanimously approved of
the mass-executions. They would have liked the executions to be
on a larger scale, because the way these took place, they weakened the secret Jewish forces only to a small extent; those Jewish elements who managed to escape are the ones who are
capable of carrying out acts of terror, and supporting the communist movement.

Hatred against Jews has not weakened. The anti-Jewish measures of the authorities prove that the danger represented by
Jews has been recognized by the government also. Consequently, they have begun to take measures against this minority.
/.../

The citizens of Romania, irrespective of their political views, act
as one when it comes to the Jewish issue. Everyone says that we
may never receive another opportunity to finally solve the Jewish
issue forever. They receive encouragement from German troops,
and from the way in which the Jewish issue has been solved in
the re-occupied territories. /.../

There is a certain dissatisfaction among Jews, perhaps because
some infectious diseases (typhoid) have broken out in the camps
where we have sent several thousand of them, a lot of whom
have died.

This situation, in other words the exclusion of Jews from a number of spheres of activity is causing rapid impoverishment; this
could be dangerous, firstly, because not even the Jewish communities can stop the further spread of misery. This may cause serious disturbances regarding public safety; Jewish tramps, mostly
children and women, whose parents and husband have disappeared, have already appeared in the streets. /.../

The Romanianization of the commercial life is continuing inten-
sively, but Romanian elements who would like to make their way
in the economy are missing. /.../

***

22.

Extract from decision No.2628

of the Bucharest Court of Justice

on June 26, 1948; First Criminal Dept.

(File No.1946/1948)

The council of judges: Ioan Paulian, Chairman; Aurel Farcutiu,
Councillor; Bella Gruia, people's assessor; Nicolae Tatu, people's assessor; Florian Pop, people's assessor.

Prosecuting magistrate: Octav Vasiliu, prosecutor; Costache
Balcu prosecuting councillor delegate; Valer Zidveanu, prosecutor delegate.

Clerk of the court: Marin Carstea

Judgement

In the name of the law, based on statute No.291 of 1947 clause
3, referring to war-criminals and those guilty of crimes committed
against peace or humanity, the court of justice convicts the following accused citizens for crimes committed, which are within
the range of the wording of the statute cited:

Sentenced to penal servitude for life, 100 million lei fine and the
suspension of their civil liberties for 10 years: General Gheorghe
Stavrescu; Colonel Dumitru Captam , Colonel Ermil Maties ; Lieu-
tenant-Colonel Constantin Ionescu Micandru; Lieutenant-Colonel
Danubiu Marinescu ; Major Gheorghe Balotescu ; Major Emil
Tulbure ; Sub-Lieutenant Eugen Mihailescu; Aurel Triandaf;
Gheorghe Cristescu; Grigore Petrovici; Gheorghe Cimpoescu;
Sergeant Vasile Mihailov; Police Constable Ion Botez;
Lance-Sergeant Mircea Manoliu; Dumitru Cercel; Gheorghe
Condurache; Dumitru Dumitriu, alias Cudi and alias Tigrel; Emil

Vivoschi; Iosub Ghita; Gheorghe Grosu; Rudolf Lubas; Dumitnu Rusu alias Gheorghe.

Life imprisonment with hard labor, 100 million lei fine and the suspension of civil liberties for 10 years: Colonel Lupu Constantin.

Penal servitude for 25 years, 100 million lei fine and the suspension of civil liberties for 10 years: Dumitru Andronic; Constantin Blandut, alias Andrei; Leon Cristiniuc; Ion Laur, alias Jorbo; Gheorghe Bocancea; Stafan Scobai;   Mihai Anitulesei.

Penal servitude for 25 years, 100 million lei fine and the suspension of civil liberties for 10 years: Dumitru Ciubotarasu;

Lazar Constantin; Nicolae Lupu; Tanase Gheorghe;   Florian Ciornei;   Dumitru Dumitriu; Manastireanu; Ion Moraru Dumitru; Alexandru   Pasarica; Gheorghe Parlafes; Vasile Velescu.

Imprisonment with hard labor for 20 years, 100 million fine penalty and the suspension of civil liberties for 10 years:

 Dumitru Constantinescu, alias Albescu.

Penal servitude for 15 years, 100 million lei fine and the suspension of civil liberties for 10 years: Dumitru Atudorei; Dumitru Dacarlat; Aurel Gramatiuc   Nicolae Miron; Nicolae Rusu; Paraschiva Barlaconschi Morosanu.

Penal servitude for 5 years, 100 million lei fine and the suspension of civil liberties for 10 years: Ion Ciobanu, otherwise Balteanu.

Proceedings against   Dumitru Popovici have ceased, since he has died.

The court of justice acquitted the following: Gheorghe Andreias, Dumitru Ghicicov,   Ion Leucea, Ion Epure.

***

23.

Ministry of the Interior

4147/June 21, 1941.

Inspectorate of the Gendarmerie

General Antonescu, Leader of the State orders the following:

1. Every healthy Jew between the age 18 and 40 must be evacuated from the villages between the Seret and Prut either to the concentration camp to Targu Jiu, or to nearby villages. The first trains must depart on June 21 this year.

Members of Jewish families who do not fall into this category, as well as other Jewish families must be evacuated from the villages of Moldova to the county towns capable of ensuring their survival; the county heads are responsible for the execution of this order.

The evacuation must be carried out within 48 hours of receipt of this letter.

Jewish families living in the other villages of the country must be evacuated to the town centres of the given county with provisions necessary for their survival; the county heads are responsible for the execution of this order; the evacuation must be carried out within 4 days of receipt of this letter. /.../

Lists of evacuees' names must be compiled and given to the police offices responsible so that the names can be registered, thus making it easier to identify Jews if they leave the place to which they have been evacuated.

Families must not return to villages from which they been evacuated.

The houses of evacuees as well as other property left behind must be handed over to the local administrative authorities. /.../

* * *

24.

Mayor's Office of Pascani town,

Baja County

Announcement

According to provisions of the order of General Antonescu,
Leader of the State, and the Ministry of Interior, No.4599/ 941,
which was forwarded by the County Head's Office of the of Baia
County with transcript No.434/941, we hereby inform everyone
that a curfew for Jewish people is now in effect. No male or female Jew is allowed to walk in the streets between 18.00 hrs and
07.00 hrs, and no persons other than family members are permitted to stay in their homes.

We also inform everyone that according to the laws mentioned
above, acts of treasons, aggression, sabotage or terror committed by Jews and their family members, or by communists or com-
munist-Iron Guards, will be punished with death penalty. The
imprisoned Jewish hostages will be the first to be executed.

Pascani, July 4, 1941.   Town Mayor A. Hanciu

***

Part 3. Transnistria

Historical Review

World War II represents the greatest degree of degradation in human civilization. Each war contains the damned germ of human barbarity. It is only natural that such a protracted confrontation of such dimensions, this universal war, which had forced powers vying for precedence to confront each other like enraged enemies, awakened age-old instincts which, once out of control, destroyed and annihilated without mercy. World War I had already shown the horrifying examples of the vile depths to which twentieth century man was capable of sinking: here we are primarily referring to the Teutons. It is enough to mention the relics of culture destroyed in Louvain and Reims, the persecution suffered by the inhabitants of occupied territories: deportation, the murder of POWs, the introduction of poisonous gases in Belgium and Northern France; the list is endless.

It was to be expected that a new confrontation capitalizing on the latest scientific developments would, in its cruelty and barbarity, surpass anything ever recorded in the history of war. Every piece of writing by experts published during the relatively calm period of 1920 -1939 predicted the cruel nature of the war to come with a sense of horror, or sometimes haughtiness. None of these publications, however, was endowed with an imagination capable of forecasting the horrifying reality experienced by mankind between 1939 and 1945.

The main victims of the barbarity which broke loose were European Jews living on territories under the occupation or influence of Germany.

In the percentage ratings the Jewish people are No.1 in the list of war victims (63% of the 9,500,000 European Jews were killed). Taking into account the total number of victims, they lie in second position behind the Soviet Union; from the point of view of suffering endured, however, theirs surpassed the suffering of any nation at any time.

It is superfluous to refer at this point to the geographically insignificant names which now instill fear, i.e. Drancy, Belsen, Buchenwald, Theresienstadt, Auschwitz, Maidanek, etc.; these will constitute individual chapters in history from now on. First among these is Transnistria.

There is no such dominion, province, county or district indicated on one single map or Geography textbook of Ukraine, Czarist Russia or the Soviet Union. Transnistria, as a geographical entry, had not existed prior to July 1941, and, of course, will never exist in the future. As the scene of an endless series of indescribable suffering, and the burial ground of hundreds of thousands of Jews, Transnlstria will remain one of the terrifying chapters in history.

For three years part of the Ukraine, the rich and fertile soil north of the Black Sea as far as the Dniester and the Bug, was known by that name. The Romanian government of Ion Antonescu was entrusted with governing and exploiting it.

Centuries of Jewish life and suffering had been linked to this land. The mystical spirit of Bal Shem, whose armchair from the synogogue in Shargorad was devoutly protected by deported Jews even when they were threatened with death from every direction, lingered over the area. It was from here that Shalom Alechem selected a great number of his protagonists, one of whom, Tobias, the milkman, was born and lived in the narrow street which still bears his name. The Biluists, the pioneers of the Jewish renaissance, passed through this land. It was also here, in the large city of Odessa, that one of the strongest Jewish intellectual centers was established; Haim Nachman Bialik, Achad Haam, Mendala Mocher Sfurim, S. M. Dubnov, M. Usiskin and the outstanding groups of thinkers and writers centered around Hasiloach and Haolam came from here.

Decades of bitter Jewish suffering are also connected with this same region. At the end of the nineteenth century the Czarist oligarchy used pogroms and anti-Semitic persecution as a pillar against democratic ideas and movements, which were on their way towards successful fruition. From 1881 onwards, the western, and particularly the southwestern part of Russia was a continually stirred cauldron of barbaric anti-Semitic hatred. In Podolia (from part of which the damned Transnistria was formed sixty years later) the pogrom in Odessa was organized, and was followed a year later (April 10, 1882) by the great pogrom in Balta, during which hundreds of Jews were beaten, tortured or murdered.

In 1900 there was another pogrom in Odessa, and a couple of years later (in 1905) one of the bloodiest slaughters of Jews was organized in the same city. And, finally, it was in this region that the Jews also had to suffer the 1917 Petljura pogroms (Odessa, Balta, Krivoje-Ozero, etc.).

The dawning of the new age proved to be bright and hopeful after this period. For almost a quarter of a century, the Jews between the Bug and the Dniester lived as human beings among human beings.

The Jews on this side of the Dniester lived in a more depressing atmosphere, a superficial and relative tranquility, constantly interrupted by the bloody and violent manifestations of hatred through mobs encouraged by the highest powers of Romania. The criminal war instigated by Adolf Hitler and Ion Antonescu revived and infinitely multiplied the agony of the past. This territory was subjugated, renamed Transnistria, and earmarked as the graveyard of local and Romanian Jews. Most of these appalling plans were carried out. Today, the soil of Transnlstria envelops the entire Jewish population of Odessa, found there by Ion Antonescu's army in October 1941, as well as a substantial proportion of Jews from villages and towns in the province. The bones of two thirds of the Jews deported from Romania in 1941 and 1942 can be found at the same place, following the murder of half of the Jews - before September 1, 1941 - living in the provinces affected by deportation (the counties of Bessarabia, Bucovina and Dorohoi).

It took until the spring of 1944 for this horrible outcome—about 350,000 dead—to be realized through murder, massacres, execution campaigns, methods of barbaric persecution, torture, looting and the conditions maintained in camps (misery, disease and hunger). The methods of murder varied extremely, and the selection included almost everything invented by the human mind from ancient times until Hitler's day.

Starting from June 1940, and lasting until March 1944, the Jews of the counties of Bessarabia, Bucovina and Dorohoi, and later the Jews of Transnistria, perished as a result of being shot to death, poisoned, hanged, drowned, slaughtered, burned, and starved to death as well as from infectious diseases, the withholding of treatment, the total weakening of the body, and torture resulting in either the death or suicide of its victims. It must be emphasized that gas chambers and upgraded crematoriums did not figure among the methods of homicide, and neither were there "scientific" experiments, i.e. vivisection, infection with viruses, the study of the resistence of the human body to extreme temperatures, etc. In connection with this, it should also be mentioned, however, that Romania is a latecomer to civilization, and lags behind when compared with the weight of German culture in Europe.

Although signs of German Nazi methods, i.e. the cynicism and fraudulence of planning, the secrecy of preparation, and the brutality of the execution, can be observed, all the actions aimed at the deportation and extermination of Jews were the work of Romanian fascism. It is also true that some of these unfortunate people fell prey to German barbarism. It is part of the truth, and must be emphasized, there were some differences in methods, and boundaries in time that Romanian authorities of higher and lower rank did not step over, or at most only sporadically so. However, the suffering of the approximately 450,000 people, of whom 350,000 died, was not the result of German demands and pressure. The bloodbaths in July and August 1941 in Bessarabia and Bucovina, which claimed the most victims, were organized by the conquering armies. Among them was the XI German army of General von Schobert. However, his authority extended only to the border of Balti county. At the other parts of the front, from Ceremus to the Danube it was only the soldiers and officers of the Romanian army who were active. The murderous perambulations in Northern Bucovina and Bessarabia, the setting up of camps in Edineti, Secureni, Vertujeni and Marculesti, as well as the deportation of the autumn of 1941, were requested by the Romanian army, approved by the highest civilian authorities, and executed by the Police and Gendarmerie. The system of looting and terror preceding the deportation as well as the events in Transnistria were organized and also executed by the Romanian authorities (governorships, county head offices, police headquarters, and Gendarme Offices). The continuously depressing and constantly threatening atmosphere was brought about through the initiative of the highest ranks of the Romanian leadership. This was further aggravated by artificially created hatred which appeared with the outbreak of the war.

The will of the Germans was the directing force behind the tragic events in Transnistria on only two occasions: during the great campaigns of massacre in 1942 and 1943, and in the deportation in the autumn of 1942.

German military and political successes reached their pinnacle in 1942, but the great turning point, which marked the beginning of the collapse of the entire fascist system, also occurred in the same year. When the Teutonic reign extended from Brest to Voroniezh and from Narvik to Tobruk; when the German armies were triumphantly approaching the Caspian Sea, the Volga and the Nile; when the Hitlerian mentality deeply engraved itself on European thought spreading throughout the continent, and encouraging the barbaric and sick psychosis of racial superiority, the national-socialist leadership decided to realize one other point of its plan: the complete extermination of European Jews. This plan also applied to Jews in Romania.

Large-scale operations were begun in the autumn of 1942 in France, Belgium, Holland, Slovakia, and especially in Poland, Belorussia and the Ukraine. The closest extermination campaign to the borders of Romania, which annihilated the entire Jewish population of this region, took place in the province of Kamenetz Podolsk (Stanislaw, Horodenka, Kolomea). This campaign extended as far as the border with Transnistria; in addition to a few thousand local Jews in the province of Bar-Jaltuska, many formerly deported Rumanian Jews were killed. For the latter the execution campaigns along the river Bug (Galsin, Krasnopolsk, Nemirov, Mihailovka, Tarasivka) were the most painful. Here, some of the victims were selected by the Germans from the camps next to the quarries in Peciora and Ladizhin (3,000 a day), and from the ghettos set up in Tulchin, Bershad, etc. Theoretically, this territory was exclusively under Rumanian authority. However, as a result of the anti-Semitic delirium, and, especially, the inferiority complex of the Rumanian authorities, German demands for the mass extradition of Jews did not meet with any resistance.

It cannot be categorically stated that this happened in the framework of a preplanned action, in which the Romanian authorities transported the Jews there, and SS troops and the Todt squads murdered them. However, events took place exactly according to this scenario, which makes complicity obvious. The highest ranks of the Romanian authorities (the Governorship of Bucovina) transported the Jews there, the lower Romanian bodies (county head offices, police headquarters, Gendarmerie Legions) handed them over, without any objection, at the request of the Germans, who in turn exterminated all of them in the framework of campaigns—lasting until the spring of 1944—organized according to national-socialist methodology.

There was one other part of Transnistria where German supremacy was able to prevail unhindered as a result of the same inferiority complex: this was Berezovca county in the province of Mostovoi- Vasilonovo-Rastadt, where an important General Command of an SS unit was operating. The Romanian authorities considered this place to be the most appropriate for the survivors of Odessa and the deportees from the Old Kingdom (historical Romania) and Transylvania. It cannot be supposed on this occasion either that there existed an earlier Romanian-German agreement. However, events occurred within the same criminal framework. On January 7, the Governor of Transnistria ordered the internment of Jews from Odessa—approx. 20,000 people—to the ghetto in Slobodtka. Later, in January and February, the Romanian Gendarmerie evacuated them to the province of Mostovoi. Starting in March, the SS troops continuously took them over and executed them in groups of a few hundred in the framework of actions lasting until autumn.

Similarily, the Romanian Leader of the State, Ion Antonescu, at the end of July 1942 ordered the deportation of a group of Jews consisting of a few hundred from the Old Kingdom and Transylvania to Transnistria; all of those who had asked for an entry visa from the Soviet Embassy in 1940. In early September the Ministry of the Interior sent them to the province of Mostovoi, where they were immediately requested, received and executed by SS troops.

Events took a totally different turn during the second German attempt in the autumn of 1942, which was aimed at the application of the national-socialist plan in Romania. The Hitlerites had taken for granted the extermination of all Jews under the authority of the Romanian government.

Nazi pressure, which had its effect on offices behind padded doors, and later manifested itself arrogantly and cynically in the foreign and German press of Bucharest, did not meet with any resistence at first. Moreover, it had Antonescu's approval from the very outset, and was looking for opportunities to co-operate with Romanian institutions in a position to carry out operations: the Joint Chiefs of Staff and the Ministry of the Interior. However, after the first groups had been despatched, and when everything was ready for the mass deportation from Transylvania and Banat, German plans collided with the characteristic Romanian bureaucracy, indecisiveness, torpor, petty interests and a certain amount of altruism, and the campaign had to be postponed at first, and later completely abandoned. /.../

This miracle has been much talked about. However, only simplistic and superficial statements have been made alleging, that while in Europe Jews were totally or almost totally exterminated, in Romania nearly all of them survived. This statement is true, but only as a premeditated assessment, which takes into account exclusively the Jews in the Old Kingdom, Transylvania and Banat.

According to the above assessment, only 10% of the Jewish population was murdered. However, if an honest study were made, considering the numbers of Jews under the jurisdiction of the Romanian state between 1941-1944, the number of those killed would exceed 50%, which far from being miraculous, is outright disastrous.

Historical facts must be disclosed. If a percentage rate cannot form the basis of such a study, absolute numbers must be taken into account. When Romania was liberated from fascist tyranny, there were approx. 300,000 Jews alive within Romanian borders, and approx. 68,000 beyond the borders. This is the miracle.

Different factors played a role in this. The most important of these are the following:

1.   Romania was not occupied militarily by Germany;

2.   The Romanian economy could not function without the services of Jews;

3.   The character and temperament of leading Romanian figures was inconsistent; they hesitated and were easily influenced;

4.   The Romanian public accepted fascist ideas only sporadically and temporarily, and the methods of fascism even less so.

In greater detail:

1.   According to their status, the sovereign states which accepted, or were forced to accept the "new European order", can be placed in two different categories:

a) Militarily occupied states; among them, France, Belgium, Holland, Norway, Czechoslovakia, Austria, Yugoslavia, Albania, Greece, Poland, Belorussia, the Ukraine, and later Italy (from September 1943), and Hungary (from March 19, 1944).

b) States under German political influence: Romania, Finland and Bulgaria (Denmark was somewhere between these two categories).

In the states listed in the first category, national-socialism was able to introduce measures directly, which were carried out by its own collaborating authorities, or by national bodies under the control of, or financed by the Gestapo. No agreement whatsoever was required for the execution of deportation and extermination campaigns, such measures could not be met with any resistence. The pogrom was carried out without delay, postponement or hesitation, and without mercy. Thanks to brave individual efforts, widely and benevolently supported by national resistance campaigns, there were some exceptions. In Italy and Hungary the persecution of Jews took on more restrained and milder forms at first, and turned into mass executions only following actual German military occupation.

Romania and Bulgaria were almost vassals under German political influence. However, they retained a certain veneer of sovereignty, and were able to show resistance in economic and racial policy spheres. At times they were even granted concessions in matters of racial policy in return for economic concessions. Consequently, the persecution and extermination of Jews in Romania was restricted to Romanian initiatives, with the Germans intervening only occasionally. That these reached extreme proportions and led to mournful results is due, on the one hand, to two decades of the psychological preparation of a sick generation, supported in its wanderings by

Rumanian pseudo-democracy, and on the other hand, to the incitement to hatred by the dictatorial leadership of the Rumanian state at the start of the "holy war". In Bulgaria, where these circumstances were not present, Hitlerite, anti-Semitic persecution caused enormous suffering, but claimed few victims.

2.   The Romanian national economy was greatly indebted to Jewish entrepreneurs for their mentality, competence and energy. There is a certain amount of truth in the then anti-Semitic statement that the proportion of Jews in leading economic positions, among specialists in technology and industrial workers, was high. However, within their sphere of activities, they did not extort but were creative. With the exception of the agricultural sector, in which they were not allowed to operate before the emancipation of 1919, in every sphere of economic life - in financial life, in industry and trade - Jews were the pioneers, who sometimes suffered the risks of taking the initiative, while at times enjoying the fruits of their persistence. It was only natural that, given this situation, economic life could not dispense with them, and could not have functioned without them.

This fact was not yet sensed by the Romanian leadership during the Iron Guard delirium. However, shortly before and during the war, it was, especially after the rapid evacuations from Bucovina. Without admitting the truth, and while legislation to remove Jews from economic life continued, the Antonescu government kept some of them on in their economic posts, and hesitated when it came to making a final decision on their total extermination.

3.   The Romanian leaders in whose power it was to decide whether Romanian Jews should live or die, were the following: Ion Antonescu, the Leader of the State; Mihail Antonescu, Vice-President of the Council of Ministers, but in reality, the Premier, and General C. Z. Vasiliu, Deputy State-Secretary of the Police and Public Order.

All three committed serious crimes against their country and against Jews. At the same time, in addition to their crimes, they did not possess the qualities required by peoples' leaders in decisive historical moments. Primarily absent in them was the belief in an ideal and the consistence in holding onto one.

Ion Antonescu was just as much of a lunatic as Mussolini and Hitler. However, he possessed neither the leadership qualities of the former nor the iron will of the latter. He was an evil man who hated people. He was especially irritated by Jews, not because he held particular convictions, but because through anti-Semitism, he was able to vent his inherent hatred. He did not like the Germans, either. He allied himself to them, sacrificed the blood of the country, its values and honor, served them with sinful loyalty, only because it was with their assistance that he was capable of fulfilling his arrogant ambitions; his pretense and passion for power.

He was a superficial man, endowed with only very limited intellectual potential. He was vain and quick-tempered. Consequently, he could be influenced both positively and negatively. He would often make contradictory decisions.

At his trial, Ion Antonescu said the following: "Thanks for the fact that there are Romanian Jews still alive is owed to Marshall Antonescu." In the very least, this statement needs to be supplemented. It expresses historical truth only to the following extent: out of the Romanian and Soviet Jews in his charge, Ion Antonescu left 350,000 alive after murdering nearly more than 350,000.

Mihail Antonescu was a fortunate careerist, positioned at the peak of the pyramid by circumstance, but because he was uneducated and lacked the spiritual qualities necessary for his station, it was his fate to plummet directly into the path of the firing squad. He was not as loyal as Ion, but slyer. He would even have sold his soul to the Germans, and served them astutely for as long as he believed in their invincibility. When he realized that they were vulnerable, he slowly distanced himself from them.

What he said during the war, and also in his confession following liberation, namely that he had never been an anti-Semite, might be true. In this case, his actions during the war, when he was one of those who provoked the barbaric and murderous hatred which led to the organization of bloodbaths at the time, seem even more despicable and burden his conscience even more heavily. He was unable to redeem himself later, when (after his visit to the Vatican in the autumn of 1943, during which he realized the prospects for the future) he attempted to ease his conscience and diminish his responsibility. He withdrew some anti-Semitic measures, prevented others from being enacted, and even saved the lives of many Jews, especially those who escaped from Hungary to Romania.

General C. Z. Vasiliu (Picky), the vigilant Minister of the Police, was an average man with ordinary human shortcomings and weaknesses. An immoral, greedy womanizer, he formulated his feelings and attitudes towards Jews in an attempt to balance his loyalty to Ion Antonescu with his own interests. He was not as sinister as his predecessor, General Popescu (Jack), whose actions were soon forgotten after his death. At first, he seemed to justify the hope attached to him by those persecuted, when he took office in January 1942. A few months later, in the autumn of 1942, he became an unmerciful executioner of Nazi plans aimed at the complete extermination of Romanian Jews.

4.   The Romanian public, which, during both the era of pseudo-democracy and the dictatorship, was confined to the views of the municipal petit bourgeoisie, to whose formation the masses of workers and peasants had not contributed to any extent, went through an interesting and particular transformation between September 6, 1940 and August 23, 1944. The public greeted Ion Antonescu with enthusiasm, tolerated - usually indifferently but also with a certain amount of disgust - the Iron Guard delirium; it did not want the war, but neither did it much oppose it. The traditional but exclusively political aspect of anti-Semitism would never have become so aggressive and lamentable (even though a generation gone astray had been inciting it for twenty years, stimulated from outside and encouraged from inside), irrespective of which political group took over the leadership of the country.

The war took the public by surprise at a time when anti-Semitic inclinations had not yet turned into outright hatred. This transformation was to occur now. From June to November of 1941, hostile manifestations increased. Nobody loathed the idea of bloodbaths - the representatives of the petit bourgeoisie even played an active part in them. They organized economic and social boycotts, watched with distaste as the marching columns of Jewish evacuees with spades and pick-axes on their shoulders were led away to public service; they insulted and physically abused those wearing yellow stars, and reacted indifferently or even enthusiastically to the deportation campaigns of the autumn of 1941. This outflow of hatred was genuine, and reached its pinnacle in October 1941, when Antonescu launched his entire propaganda machine in order to justify crimes already committed and provide encouragement for those yet to come. At the time, public opinion was prepared to give credit to any gossip; hesitation was entirely abandoned, and hatred took over in almost everyone.

Two months later, the Jews forced to shovel snow, were greeted with bread and hot meals. However, the decline of hatred was slower than its rise. In any case, it proved to be enough for the public not to remain totally indifferent to the campaign aimed at complete extermination. The manifestation of good-will on the part of the population resulted in a hesitant and delaying approach from those who took part in the ordinary, but nevertheless historic meeting of the Council of Ministers on October 13, 1942. The Allied Armies did the rest a month later at El Alamein, Algiers and Stalingrad.

However, while "the miracle" was happening on both sides of the Carpathian Mountains, in that country blessed by God, but cursed by human evil, in that enormous camp enclosed by the wide and deep waters of the Dniester and the Bug, the painful tale of Jews deported from Romania drew to its fateful close. Approx. 120,000 people were dragged there. The land of Transnistria was to become their den, its soil their food, and its earth their grave. From the first day to the last, the murderous scorning of Jews continued.

"We brought you here to die. We would still like to ask you to prevent the spread of infectious diseases.", said the physician sent to Moghilev by the governorship.

"Are there any living Jews left in Transnistria?", the governor of the province asked his subordinates innocently from time to time.

"Only the total extermination of these evil-doers and fanatic communists can free mankind from the danger of communism", the Inspector of the Transnistrian Gendarme reported to his superiors, while requesting further orders.

From high-ranking officials to the last camp guard, nobody missed a chance to prove in words or deeds that the great task at hand was the total extermination of Jews.

While Transnistria does not call to mind the apocalyptic flames of crematoriums, the methods which served the eventual realization of the objective were nevertheless frighteningly versatile. They serve as an example of methodic mass execution. Here, the undermining of the victims' moral stamina overshadowed the physical torture. In German camps victims quickly grew apathetic, so terribly so that not only did they give up all hope at the very beginning, but completely ceased to exist as moral beings. In Transnistria the hope was constantly alive in them, they were always aware of the gradual degradation humanness, and accurately experienced the truly terrifying moral pains. The fear of all sorts of diseases that threatened them from all sides; the problem of providing food for themselves and their loved ones, the horror of being beaten or tortured, to which they were constantly exposed - with or without pretext; the continuous anxiety over the threat of transportation to camps within the country or beyond the Bug, paralyzed their senses, numbed their physical pain, but enormously increased their moral suffering.

The most important contributory causes of the physical and psychological annihilation of the Jews deported to Transnistria were, naturally, the above-mentioned (disease, hunger, torture, deportation or the nightmares of these). The fact that total extermination could not be achieved can be attributed to another "miracle", brought about by the enormous vitality and indefatigable energy of the Jews. A small group of people—sometimes one single person—were capable of creating a community from the mass of uprooted, exhausted suffering and persecuted people, through initiative, courage, strong will, stamina, and the power of respect as well as Jewish solidarity.

Leaders emerged, unelected, unappointed and unconfirmed in their roles.

Similarly, Jewish institutions sprang up in a spontaneous and natural way as a consequence of necessity and tragedy. The Office of Organizing Jewish Work can be considered one of these. Such institutions were widely disdained by Jews, who saw that such organizations could be used as tools by the enemy. These notorious offices played the role of necessary evil by eliminating unjust actions and hindering brutal acts of persecution. Because of the general hunger, public eateries, communal kitchens and food distribution centers had to be set up, and the wonderful industrial 'associations' (construction or small-scale industry workshops) had to be organized. Because of the epidemics, primarily the petechial typhus, dilapidated buildings had to be transformed into hospitals, and an excellent health service had to be created out of nothing, which, in spite of, or above the heads of, the inefficient or malicious authorities, started a gigantic battle against the disease, and was victorious over it.

Orphanages, kindergartens and primary schools were established, because the depressing sight of parent-less, dirty, ragged and exhausted children roaming the streets begging, or perishing along the roads, was unacceptable.

Slowly, with human sacrifices, and primitive and empirical methods, from dust, blood and soot the wonder of society in Transnistria came into existence: the formation of an organized community out of a debased and directionless crowd In less than six months, and in spite of disease, hunger and misery, the level of Transnistrian Jewish organization became state-like, winning the admiration of the persecutors, and at times, altering their mentality, or substituting their authority.

(...) Thanks to the energetic attitude of Jews, the Transnistrian "miracle" came about, which despite disease and human evil, saved the lives of approx. 60,000 Jews; at the time of liberation there were 15,000 local Jews among them.

The Red Army liberated Transnistria in early March 1944. The Soviet troops, which had set out from Uman county on March 10, crossed the Bug on March 16, and reached the bank of the Dniester in a mere four days. The speed of the attack, which dispersed the fascist troops and forced them to flee chaotically, preempted the final danger. The tired bodies and broken bones of the survivors of the Transnistrian hell had been saved. /.../

The Massacres in Bessarabia, Bucovina and Dorohoi County

The Chronological Order of Events

June 2, 1940 - November 15, 1941

June 1940

Approximately 800,000 Jews were living in Greater Romania before the war. According to the last official census on December 19, 1930, there were 756,930 people. More than one third of these (314,933) lived in the counties of Bessarabia, Bucovina and Dorohoi.

Note: According to a survey carried out by the Central Statistical Office on September 1, 1941, after the first two months of the war, only 151,121 of this number had survived.

The racially based census taken on May 20, 1942 indicated that only 19,576 Jews were living in these counties. However, in the so-called "Transnistrian" camps and ghettos about 60,000 people were alive at this time.

June 29, 1940

In accordance with the execution of the agreement on the handover of Bessarabia and the northern Bucovina region, as well as a number of settlements in Dorohoi county, the withdrawal of Romanian troops began along the entire length of the border from the Ceremus to the Danube. It seems that the troops which withdrew across the bridges of the Prut from Galati to Herta, were composed and behaved decently. In any case, no extraordinary events were recorded concerning them. However, the troops which withdraw to Bucovina after crossing the Prut and the Siret, committed horrible crimes and terrifying massacres, which claimed the lives of a great number of Jewish villagers and townspeople.

The first murders were committed in Mihoreni (Dorohoi county) by a military unit under the command of a major named Gilav. For no apparent reason, the soldiers arrested and tortured Sloime Weiner, his son, User Weiner, his daughters, Roza Weiner and Fani Zekler (the latter was holding a two-year-old child in her arms). They were taken to a forest called Tureatca, where a lame cobbler, Moscovici, his wife and two children, as well as Isac Moscovici's wife and two daughters were also found. All of them were lined up at the edge of a hole and shot into it. Isac Moscovici, who had been arrested separately, was so severely beaten that he died on the way to hospital.

June 30, 1940

Part of the 16th infantry regiment, under the command of Major Valeriu Carp, withdrew from the north-western part of Bucovina towards Falticeni. Immediately after the unit had marched into the village of Ciudei (Strojinet county), a number of Jews were collected at the village center following an order by the Major. These were: Moise Schachter, Dr. Konrad Kreis, the Hessman brothers, Herman Gross, his wife, his daughter and grandchild. All of them were shot dead. Dr. Kreis was tortured with extraordinary cruelty, and his body was - literally - cut up into pieces.

June 30, 1940

A group of 18 soldiers, led by a lieutenant, broke into the house of Suhar Lax, who lived in Costina-Suceava. After torturing him, they tied him to a horse's tail and had him dragged across the village (nearly 3 km). His body, ridden with twenty bullets, was found in a nearby forest.

July 1, 1940

The withdrawing military units carried out a barbaric and murderous pogrom in the town of Dorohoi.

The morning streets of the city showed signs of extraordinary activity, and the Jews of the town began to panic. The soldiers of the 8th Rifle Regiment, who were not acquainted with the city, led by locals, were roaming the city center and the Jewish quarter, marking Christian houses with large "C" letters. A consequence of the activity of the soldiers, or because they were secretly encouraged to do so, many Christians put crosses and icons in their windows. The soldiers mocked, jeered and abused the small number of Jews who crossed their path.

The funeral of a Jewish soldier, who had died during a border incident near Herta, was taking place around noon. Many leading personalities of the local Jewish community insisted on bowing before the grave of their hero, and decided to pay their last respects to him. The Dorohoi garrison sent a guard of honor consisting of ten Jewish soldiers to the Jewish cemetery. There was also a cadet sergeant among them, but he was not the commander of the guard of honor, who was a Christian sergeant.

At around 2.00 p.m., when the coffin was being lowered into the grave, shots could be heard from the western part of the cemetery. This was the signal for the pogrom; it was rumored in the town that the Jews had opened fire at the army. The sergeant ordered the Jewish soldiers to leave the cemetery, while the other terrified Jews fled to the funeral parlor. At the gate of the cemetery the Jewish soldiers were met by a colonel, some officers and a platoon. The colonel gave the order to disarm and execute the Jewish soldiers, who only ten minutes before had been members of a guard of honor of the Romanian army. They were placed in row facing the wall of the cemetery and shot from behind by their comrades in full view of the colonel.

Events continued in the funeral parlor. A lieutenant, with a pistol in his hand, kicked in the door, and under the pretext of searching for people with arms, chased the terrified Jews out of the parlor, who then witnessed the horrible execution. They were lined up along Valea Campului Street (8 women, a two-year-old, a six-year-old, a seven-year-old child, and an eighty~year-old man among them), and murdered with a few rounds of machine-gun fire. The bullets missed the old man, so they smashed his skull with a sharp blow. Some of the people survived by either running away across the field or by pretending to be dead.

Simultaneously with the bloodbath organized in the cemetery, the pogrom began in the town. In Regele Ferdinand, Bratianu and C. Stroici Streets the soldiers forced their way into Jewish houses, tortured, looted and murderd. Never before had Romanian soil witnessed such bestial scenes. Avram Calmanovici was shot dead, but only after his genitals had been cut off. The elderly Eli and Feiga were shot dead, but first the woman's ears were cut off for the sake of her earrings. The breasts of Ms. Rifca Croitoru were cut off. The elderly Herscu Iona's beard was pulled out hair by hair, and only then was he shot dead.

The pogrom was brought to a close by a huge rainstorm, which drove the soldiers off the streets.

The Jewish soldiers of 24th Infantry Regiment were also close to being murdered, but this was averted by a courageous intervention (perhaps that of Captain Stino).

The massacre in the provinces was also averted through the actions of General Sanatescu and Colonel Ilasievici. However, two other Jewish soldiers were shot dead near the town of Mihaileni. They were later buried by the local religious community. In Valea Campului, two more Jewish soldiers, who had come from a military unit to visit their children, were also killed.

July 1, 1940

The troops under the command of Valeriu Carp arrived in Zaharesti in Suceava county, where they rested. There was one Jew in the village. The major ordered the collection of a larger group from the surrounding areas. A number of Jews were brought in from Vorniceni, Ilisesti, Vicov and Banila, including the following: Leon Hamer, Leib Stekel, Ira Lupovici, Nuta Druckman, Moise Haller, Bartfeld, Herer, Edelstein, mother and daughter, Dr. Gingold from Vicov, as well as a few Jews evacuated from Radauti county, who were bound for Suceava. A total of thirty-six. All of them were horribly tortured, some of them had ears, fingers or tongues cut off. Finally, they were lined up beside a hole, fired on, and thrown into the hole, irrespective of whether they were dead or still alive. The major ordered the two Jewish soldiers under his command to be included in the firing squads, one of them was from Burdujeni, the other from Suceava (Fredi Dermer). The major's daughter also took part in the massacre. The beast of a major ordered the carcass of a horse to be thrown on the mass grave of dead bodies as a final act of abuse. /.../

Encouraged by the barbarity of the soldiers, the gangs of peasants and Gendarmes also looted and murdered. In Serbauiti (Suceava county), Sergeant Bujica, the Commander of the Gendarme post, together with a peasant called Hapinciuc, who worked in the Revenue Office, broke into the house of a Jew named Smil Gheller, where, in addition to the above, were his wife, Sally Gheller, and Leib Ellenbogen. They shot all three of them, and threw their bodies into the creek beside the village. These corpses were also buried in the Jewish cemetery in Suceava in January 1941.

July 3-5, 1940

Similar crimes were committed along the entire route of the army's withdrawal:

> In Comonesti-Suceava, the Zisman siblings were shot dead after being thrown out of a train. Rabbi Laib Schachter and his two sons were first tortured, and then murdered on the edge of the village. The rabbi's wife was shot dead while at prayer. Sloime Mendler was bayoneted in the nape;
> In Crainiceni (Radauti county), the Aizic siblings and Burah Wasserman were shot dead by a group of eight soldiers led by an infantry sergeant;
> Mendel Weinstein, Maratiev and Strul Feigenbaum were murdered in Adancata;
> Moise Rudich, landowner, in Gaureni-Suceava;
> Natan Somer in Liuzii-Humorului (Suceava county);
> M. Hibner, his wife and son, Iosub Hibner, and his four grandchildren were killed by soldiers and peasants in Igesti-Suceava.

A great number of murders were committed on trains, especially along the tracks of Moldova. The Jewish passengers, primarily soldiers, were shot dead, and their corpses left in the fields. A large number of Jews were thrown out of moving trains: some of them died painful deaths, others were left crippled.

February 1941

The agreement stipulating the handover of Bessarabia and Bucovina made it possible for people from returned territories to cross the border to the other side. The most important crossing points were in Galatii-Reni and Dornesti (Bucovina). In this latter province, in Burdujeni, a Russian-Romanian joint committee had been in operation, which had ceased its activities in January, when the border was closed. The Christians who had not reached the other side by that time were sent across later, and a camp of sorts was set up for the 110 Jews who had not crossed the border (two rooms at the Burdujeni railway station). Here, they lived in horrifying poverty, a few poor Jews from Burdujeni and Suceava fed them out of pity. At times, during the the night, groups of twenty or thirty Jews were taken away; border guards took them to the border and forced them, at gunpoint, to cross the border. The frontier zone was mined, and consequently, a great number of Jews fell victim to explosions. Others were killed by the bullets of Soviet border guards alerted by the border violations. And, finally, there were those who were shot dead by Romanian border guards whilst trying to return.

In this way, by February, only fifty-eight Jews remained out of the original 110. They suffered there until May, when they were able to leave the hell of Burdujeni; they were transported to the camp in Targu Jiu.

June 30, 1941

One of the decrees of the General Command, according to which Jews had taken part in violent crimes including espionage, sabotage and attacks against individual soldiers, was an incitement to pogroms, through its order to the commanders of large units, together with their troops, to be "unmerciful" (see Doc.4).

July 2, 1941

The attack along the entire length of the Romanian border begins, from Bucovina to the Danube, simultaneously, a campaign is launched, during which looting and slaughter among the Jews occur on a massive scale along the path of the fascist army. The acts of looting and murder, both individual and mass, are committed by Romanian and German soldiers, as well as civil authorities and local residents. The simultaneousness and similarity of the crimes indicate that they were executed in accordance with pre-prepared orders and plans.

The border village of Ciudei was one of the first settlements to be occupied. At this site, one year previously, the withdrawing batteries of the 16th Infantry Regiment, under the command of Valeriu Carp, had organized a barbaric massacre. There were only a few victims then. This time, however, the soldiers of the same regiment, with the same order and the same beast of a commander, exterminated the entire Jewish population with fire and sword. In only a few hours, 450 of the 500 Jewish villagers were shot dead.

July 4, 1941

Strorojinet was the first town to be occupied. Hardly had the soldiers marched in, than the slaughter began. Women, men, the elderly and children collected at random from houses, cellars, churches and streets, were either shot dead immediately, or only after being tortured. Some names:

Solomon Drimer, the former Vice-President of the Religious Community; his daughter-in-law, Jenni Drimer; the wife of Moritz Loebel, shot dead with her child in her arms (her husband hanged himself when he learnt of this); Mendel Schmeltzer, (shot dead together with his wife and son-in-law); Moses Iuhrman and his wife; David Greif; Simon Schefler; Smiel Fleischer and his son, Leon Fleischer; Mrs. Siegler and her daughter; Fienstein and his wife and daughter; Liebman and his wife; Baruch Altman; an elderly woman (Sonntag) was executed under the pretext that she had fired on the soldiers; a nasty farce was played out at her expense; a machine-gun belt was tied to her waist, and then a photograph was taken of her; Peisah Aufleger; Coblig, the cobbler; Russ, the tailor; Mrs. Moses; Berta Leder; Schulman; M. Surchis and his wife and sons; Buci Rosner and her father-in-law, Goldberg; his daughter, Blima, was only injured, but died two days later.

July 4, 1941

In the villages near Storojinet (Ropcea, Iordanesti, Patrauti, Panca and Broscauti), the occupying troops looted and murdered the Jewish population with similar barbarity.

In Ropcea, the entire family of Osias Wolf Hass is murdered. Soldiers occupying the village enjoy themselves thoroughly. They collect everybody from Hass's house, and drive them towards Siret. Old Hass is blind, and his son, Eugen, carries him on his back during the three-kilometer walk. When they reach the river, the valiant invaders force the victims to cross the water in single file on a narrow bridge. The blind man led the way, and the soldiers had great fun watching him stumble. The old man managed to get as far as the middle of the bridge, where he was shot dead, and his body fell into the water. Next in line was Rifca Schneider, with her baby in her arms. The baby was probably still alive when its mother fell off the bridge. Then all the others, one after the other, Eugen Hass, his wife, his son and daughter. (...) The little girl was only injured, and was taken to a nearby house. However, when she came to two days later and remembered the tragedy she had experienced, she asked one of the soldiers to shoot her. Her request was granted.

Also in Ropcea, the Meer siblings and Osias Rosen—among them the brother of Rabbi Dr. Mark from Chernovitz as well as his wife.

In Iordanesti, the local residents, under the leadership of Telefon-Halache, organized a bloodbath. Among many others, the following were tortured and killed; Michel Donenfeld, Haller and his two sons, Wolloch and Heinich.

July 5, 1941

In Banila pe Siret, local residents, led by Mayor Mocaliuc and a certain Barbaza, killed 15 Jews, among them M. Satran, an eighty-year-old blind man, Iacob Fleischer and Iacob Brecher together with his daughter. Brecher's body was cut into pieces, and his blood was smeared on the axles of carriages.

Having seen so many atrocities, the priest of the Orthodox Church, Stefanovici, the pastor of Banila, did not set foot in his church the following Sunday.

July 5, 1941

The invading army organized massacres in the villages inhabited by Jews throughout Storojinet county. Eighty people were shot dead in Stanesti, among them Rabbi Friedlaender and his two sons. In Jadova Noua dozens of Jews were tortured and killed, among them Weiss Moise, his child and siblings, Weiss David and Weiss Urci.

In Jadova Veche, Rabbi Ghinsberg survived after his beard was pulled out, his head was injured in several places, and he was repeatedly bayoneted. However, Eli Schnitter and his wife, Bubi Engel, was shot dead. Many girls were raped, and the beard of every old man was cut off. It will never be known how many Jews were killed on that day, and how many later. Very few witnesses survived. The only certainty is that from among the 543 Jewish inhabitants of the two Jadovas only 80 survived the massacre and the death march to the camps in Edineti and Transnistria.

In Costesti and Hunita fewer than forty of the 400 Jews survived, the rest were killed; in Budineti, 6 out of the 8 Jewish residents were killed, among them Isidor Berghof, the Secretary of the Religious Community in Storojineti (his eyes were torn out of their sockets before he was shot dead); it is not known for certain how many Jews were killed in Cires in addition to the Jungmann family, but their blood could be clearly seen in the dust of the road when the marching column of Jews from Banila passed there. In Valavca, on the instigation of a peasant called Curichi, Zeida Krigsman, Ioil Kluger, Aron Burman and his son, Bert Daubert, Zissu Lux, his wife and one of his sons, Haiche Dermer, Stembrecher and his wife; in Milie, Dr. Iacob Geller, the leading Zionist, who was fleeing from Chernovitz, was shot dead together with his wife and one of his chidren, as well as the five member Mehrman family, which was bayoneted to pieces.

July 5, 1941

Following an order given by the Chief of Police in Herta, 100 Jews were collected from cellars and synagogues (to where they had fled), and executed. The corpses were buried in three mass graves.

On the same day, in the village of Horbova, in Herta county, the 10 local Jews were killed.

July 5, 1941

When the Romanian army marched into the town of Vijnita, 21 Jews were executed.

The Romanian troops that occupied the town called Vascauti, took 19 hostages. Their names: Dughi Wasserman, P.Haber, Leib Zeltzer and his son, Reicher and his son, Slotschewer, Machel and Ioil Singer, Strulovici, Gensler, Riezeher, Mechlovici, Engelberg, Reichman, Hans Erdreich, Moise Teller, Mendel Enzelberg and Fischel Papst. After a few hours all of them were shot dead.

July 5, 1941

In Rostachi-Vijnita, almost all the Jews were slaughtered. Ten out of 81 survived, including Dr. Stier, his wife and a child, who had fainted and were thought to be dead. The massacre was organized by local residents led by the Scimsinschi brothers, Mihai and Matae, and supported by Romanian soldiers.

July 5, 1941

The advance guards of the Romanian army marched into Chernovitz between 16.00 and 17.00 hrs. Some specially assigned units occupied strategically important positions and public buildings, while the rest flooded the Jewish quarter; the looting and killing began immediately.

July 6, 1941

The Romanian troops, which the previous day had occupied Edineti, start the massacre of the Jewish population. In two days, approx. 500 Jews were killed. Jewish women and girls were raped. Some of them committed suicide as a result.

July 6, 1941

In Noua Suli, which had been occupied by Romanian troops before the attack was launched, the authorities raided the area and set up their headquarters; upon their orders 60 Jews were selected from the camp set up in the distillery and immediately executed.

July 6, 1941

In Chernovitz, individual soldiers and patrols continued to kill Jews at random throughout the night.

The entry of the bulk of Romanian troops into the town began at dawn Some units flooded the lower part of the city, the Jewish quarter. The massacre there spread everywhere. In Romana, Calugareni, Cuciurul Mare, and other streets, soldiers went from house to house, killing all the Jews, young and old, without exception.

In less than twenty-four hours, more than 2,000 Jews were killed in the streets, yards, houses, cellars or attics, where the unfortunate were seeking refuge.

The corpses were transported in rubbish carts to the Jewish cemetery, and buried in four enormous common graves.

While the pogrom was in progress, Gendarme patrol units searched Jewish houses in the center of the town, especially in Iancu Zotta, Dimitrie Petrino, Miron Costin, and other streets. Approx. 3,000 Jews—men, women and children—were collected and shut into the cellar of the Gendarmerie Station. The Gendarmes, under the leadership of Major Cicondel, were engaged all night in abusing and torturing them. Late at

night, the women were barbarically searched - the search also involved
their genitalia. All of them were subsequently released together with the
children. Naturally, all their valuables were confiscated. /.../

In the meantime, Jews were prohibited from going out into the street.
Milk sellers and greengrocers were also forbidden to enter Jewish houses.

July 7, 1941

In Edineti, the Jews killed the day before were gathered and buried in three
mass graves. Then, the grave diggers, who were all Jewish, were also
executed.

The Jews were prohibited from going to the market, or having any contact
with the Christian population.

July 7, 1941

Following in the footsteps of German troops occupying Targu Parlit (Balti
county), a few soldiers of the 5th Romanian Infantry Regiment also crept
into the town. Their first act was to seek and loot Jewish homes. In the
house of Chidale Felder (22 Main Street), they found 10 Jews in the cellar;
the soldiers demanded money and valuables from them. After the looting
had ended, the soldiers shot all ten on the spot; four died instantly, two
sometime later. It seems that the remaining four also died. After the Romanian soldiers, one of whom was later identified by two officers, had left, the
local residents set out to loot the houses of the other Jews.

Note: The Command Center of the 11th German Army informed the Romanian High Command of the massacre and looting. An inquiry was
launched, which was conducted by the Balti Gendarmerie Legion on August 7: it concluded that other Jews had also been killed, but by German
soldiers. The inquiry, naturally, was carried out in such a way that no one
was found guilty, and no one was punished.

July 7, 1941

In the village of VIad (Balti county), peasants armed with sticks and scythes attacked the houses into which part of the Jewish population of the town of Balti had fled after June 26. The Jews were dragged out of the houses, all of them beaten, some killed, and the houses burnt to the ground.

July 8, 1941

The old Jewish settlements of Briceni and Licani were destroyed by the passing hoards. It could not be established and will never be known how many Jews were killed there on that day.

July 8, 1941

One of the units of the 14th Romanian Infantry Regiment, consisting of 20 soldiers, and led by a corporal, which had fallen behind, came across a group of 50 Jews (42 adults and 6-8 children) between the villages of Taura Veche and Taura Noua, on its way to Falesti-Chiscareni (Balti county). After everything had been taken away from them (including clothes and shoes), they were forced into a swamp, where they had to lie face down; they were shot in this position. The children were beaten to death. Only two women survived, they were found by German soldiers, who took them to hospital.

Note: It is curious that the bestial bloodletting revolted even the German soldiers who were following Romanian units. The Command Center of the 11th German Army informed the Romanian High Command of the massacre, pointing out that "the behavior of certain representatives of the Romanian army serves no other purpose than to destroy the credibility of the Romanian army, and at the same time, that of the German army in the eyes of world opinion.

The inquiry ordered by the High Command was held on August 9, 1941, by the Balti Gendarme Legion. However, no conclusions were reached.

July 8, 1941

Romanian troops occupying Marculesti (Soroca county), collected the entire Jewish population—men, women and children—and took them to the edge of the village. In the early hours of the occupation, 18 Jews, including the rabbi, were declared hostages, and shot dead. Then, the massacre began, claiming approx. 1,000 Jewish lives. The corpses were buried in the anti-tank ditches at the edge of the village.

One day after the departure of Soviet troops, but still before the arrival of Romanian troops, locals, supported by the residents of nearby villages, destroyed and looted the houses of Jews.

Similar massacres were also committed by the Romanian army in Floresti, Gura Kamenitz and Gura Cainari.

Note: Markulesti was an old Jewish agricultural settlement. Before the war, it was inhabited by 2,300 Jews and 200 Romanians, the latter forming the staff of the Parish Hall, the Revenue Office, the Gendarme Station, etc. /.../

July 11, 1941

In Lipcani-Hotin, the Military Police took 12 Jewish hostages, and subsequently executed them.

Also taken hostage and executed were 40 Jews in Lincauti-Hotin. They were buried outside the village of Muanet.

In Ceplauti-Hotin all the Jews (approx. 160 people) were killed... /.../

July 12, 1941

In Climauti-Soroca, 300 Jewish men, women and children were killed. The corpses were buried at the edge of the village. /.../

July 17, 1941

The German and Romanian troops marched into Kishinev. Along the two routes of their entry, through Sculeni from the north, and Hancesti from the south, they carried out a horrible bloodbath. The exact number of victims is not known, nor will it ever be established. However, on the basis of the number of survivors ghettoized a few days later, the number of Jews killed during the occupation of the city can be estimated at approx. 10,000.

July 25, 1941

A consignment of 25,000 Jews is transported across the Dniester to the Ukraine. Part of it arrives in Coslar, where the Jews have to wait in an open field in horrifically crowded conditions. No one is allowed to leave. A Jew and his three children are shot dead after moving a little to one side.

August 1, 1941

Upon the orders of the Gestapo, 450 Jews are selected from the ghetto in Kishinev, primarily intellectuals and pretty women. They are taken to Visterniceni next to the city, where 411 are shot dead. The surviving 39 are taken back to the ghetto in order to report the story. /.../

August 2, 1941

Those Bessarabian Jews who were taken across the Dniester were wandering along the roads of the Ukraine in miserable conditions before being transported to Moghilau. By the time the arrived, 4,000 of the original 25,000 were missing. Some may have hidden in Ukrainian villages, but a great number perished as a result of starvation and misery, and an even larger number were shot dead.

August 4, 1941

The first consignment of the Jews driven out of Storojinet arrived in Atachi, where they were supposed to cross the Dniester in order to arrive in

Moghilev. The consignment of 300 people is guarded by a corporal and two soldiers. The German authorities do not allow them to cross the Dniester; consequently, the consignment is lined up again to return to Chernovitz. After passing through a village called Volcinet, the column is stopped beside a signal box at 21.30 hrs and the people are taken off the carts together with their possessions. The Jews are divided into groups of ten, and the first group is shot into the Dniester. Following their execution, the corporal promises to allow the others to live if they hand over their money and jewelry to him. One hundred rings, and also necklaces, chains, earrings and 15,000 lei were collected and handed over to the corporal. Then, all the Jews were forced into the Dniester, and shot. A number of Jews, 60 according to some witnesses, 90 according to others, who were not hit by bullets, and could swim, survived. /.../

Note: An inquiry was launched into this massacre and its circumstances, with the aim of finding those guilty. However, the Supreme Military Judge, General Topor, decided to shelve the case.

August 6, 1941

The Jews who had been transported across the Dniester were taken to Scazinet. The old, the sick and the completely exhausted—approximately 1,000 people—were selected. They were told that they would be taken to a resting camp. All of them were shot dead, and their corpses buried in an anti-tank ditch.

August 6, 1941

Gendarmes from the 23rd Gendarme Company executed 200 Jews, and threw their bodies into the Dnester.

Note: The Gendarme Supervisory Body laconically reported this case (Report No.80, August 13). No mention was made of either the circumstances or the location of the mass massacre. At that time, the 23rd Gendarme Company was operating in Lapusna county (Kishinev).

The Supreme Military Judge, General Topor, recorded the following decision to the above report: "into the files".

August 7, 1941

Upon the orders of the Romanian authorities, a road inspector selected 500 Jews from the ghetto in Kishinev in order to take them to the Ghidignici work site. He also took 25 women to cook for the men. After a week, 200 completely exhausted people, who were physically incapable of work, returned. The remaining 325 had disappeared forever. /.../

August 9, 1941

According to the minutes signed by SS Untersturmfuhrer Frohlich and Ion Gh. Vetu, Captain of the Gendarme Legion in Chilia, it can be proven that the former conveyed an order to the latter in the name of General Antonescu, stipulating that the Gendarme Captain was to execute all the Jews (451) in the Tataresti camp (Chilia county), which was under his command.

The captain reported that the order had been carried out.

Note: There are other documents—in addition to the above-mentioned minutes—which bear witness to this massacre. One of these, for example, is a report compiled by a committee investigating certain aspects of the bloodbaths in Bessarabia during the time of Antonescu. This report also mentions the 451 murdered Jews, while other documents refer to 115 victims. It is an indisputable fact, however, that a trial was launched against the perpetrator of these murders, Captain Ion Gh. Vetu; not because he had murdered a few hundred innocent people, but because this time he had robbed them; he stole a couple of watches, rings and some money. /.../

September 1, 1941

In accordance with a directive issued by the Romanian authorities, the Central Statistical Office conducted a census in Bessarabia and Northern Bucovina. The census showed a number of 126,434 Jews in these two provinces. According to data of the previous official census, 274,036 Jews had lived on this territory.

We can conclude that two months after the commencement of military actions, at the end of the first phase of the "holy war", following the occupation of the territories which had been handed over in 1940, approx. 150,000 Jews were missing. These were either killed or perished as a result of bestial persecution, starvation, thirst, their untreated diseases and wounds, and fatigue.

September 16, 1941

The deportation to Transnistria of the Jews collected in the camps of Northern Bucovina began. A month later, following the establishment of the new camps, the counting of those interned was carried out with extreme care In certain camps (Secureni and Edineti), two counts were taken: one by military organizations, the other by village authorities. When the marching columns were started, nobody bothered to count the number of survivors.

A great number of Jews died in the camps of Secureni, Edineti, Vertujeni and Marculesti, especially in the latter two. They perished for many reasons, but all were a consequence of the horrifying conditions to which the victims had been subjected. By the end of the terrible walk, which for some lasted as long as two months, people's physical and psychological resistance had evaporated. There were some cases of suicide and premature birth at the very beginning. However, with the passing of time, the number of these grew daily. Soon the diseases caused by misery appeared:

Enteric fever, petechial typhus, scabies, dysentery, etc. Although there were many physicians among those interned, the epidemics continued to spread, and the death rate rose rapidly, since medication and the necessary medical accessories (soap, petroleum, water) were absent. Many of those who had not fallen victim to disease, died as a result of starvation and thirst. In certain places, food was totally absent, while in others there was plenty, but it was too expensive for the impoverished people. They reached the point when they gave a watch for a loaf of bread, a blanket for two loaves, and ten shirts for a bucket of water. At times camp commanders cut off the food supply lines by prohibiting peasants from entering the camp, or the Jews from leaving it.

The lack of water usually caused cruel suffering, and often death. In the camp in Edineti, there was only one well with water suitable for drinking, the water in the other well was contaminated. Most of the internees there drank rainwater, which they collected in two holes. A group of Jews left in the forest in Barnova for eight days in the middle of August had no supplies of any food whatsoever, because the peasants were prohibited from approaching them; they drank rainwater. At the beginning of September, 70-100 Jews died daily in Edineti. Some died of thirst: Pavel Grun (Stanesti), Haim Cohn (Jadova), Itic Birkenfeld (Seletin), Malca Menases, etc.

In the camps—especially in Vertujeni and Marculesti—Jews often died as a result of exhausting work, but primarily, beatings and torture. Some were killed, shot dead, purely at the whim of the commanders of the camps.

November 15, 1941

The first phase of the deportations had ended. The camps in Bessarabia as well as the ghetto in Kishinev had been emptied. Not a single Jew remained in the towns and villages of Bucovina, with the exception of Chernovitz, where 20,000 Jews were allowed to stay. At the gates to Transnistria (Moghilev, Iampol, Rabnita, Tiraspol, Iasca), the deportees were counted. It turns out from the summary report of the Transnistrian Gendarme Supervisory Body that 118,847 Jews were taken across the Dniester. Among them were the 35,000 Jews who had been deported from the counties of Southern Bessarabia and Dorohoi. The official census of September 1 showed 126,434 Jews in Bessarabia and Northern Bucovina, including the 20,000 Jews who had not been deported from Chernovitz. If the appropriate calculations are made, it turns out that during the following two months after the census a further 22,000 Jews died in Bessarabia.

A number of them died, because the starvation, thirst, misery and the suffering in the camps continued.

Others died of exhaustion on their way to the Dniester. In one of the marching columns heading towards the village of Corbu from Edineti, 860 people died during one single night near Atachi. Although it was only

November 15, it was freezing, and the first snow fell in the middle of the night. The people were almost naked, some wore rags or pieces of paper, their physical resistance had weakened considerably, and consequently the freezing conditions were easily able to finish them off. /... /

However, most of the Jews were killed by accompanying Gendarmes and "paramilitaries" (members of a paramilitary youth organization—the Editor). The roads leading from the camps towards the Dniester—primarily those from Vertujeni to Cosauti., from Marculesti to Rezina, and from Kishinev to Orhei—were literally lined with corpses. One of the instructions concerning deportation was that those lagging behind had to be shot. In addition to this, those escorting the columns killed many Jews out of whims, sadism or at the request of peasants standing by the roadside, who bought the living people for 1,500-2,000 lei, and then had them shot by the soldiers so that they could take off their clothes. /...../

After November 15, 1941,

not a single Jew was killed in Bessarabia: there were none left.

Camps and Ghettos in Bessarabia

Chronological Order of the Events

June 21, 1941 - November 10, 1941

The Minister of the Interior, in the name of General Antonescu, orders the internment of Jews from the area between the Siret and the Prut. All healthy Jewish men between the age of 16 and 60 are to be interned to the camp of Targu-Jiu, women and children to the towns. /..../

The evacuation took place among barbaric conditions. Jews had to leave their wealth behind within a few hours (in Dorohoi beside the Siret within 2 hours), they were allowed to bring as much as they could carry on their back during a ten-kilometre walk. In cattle freight carriages crowded to suffocation—sometimes these were even sealed—they were wandering about for days in the end-of-July heat without being able to get food, get out to relieve nature or look after patients.

After the evacuation of Jews, the authorities and local inhabitants completely robbed the ownerless houses, they took everything: goods, furniture, household equipment. They carried away the wealth of one or more generations until the last chair or pillow, in certain places even the doors and windows, and the tin from the roofs. Not even cemeteries were safe from the angry looting or demolition.

In territories which were later affected by deportations (Southern Bucovina and Dorohoi county) Jews were evacuated from the following places:

From the county town of Dorohoi almost every Jewish men between the ages of 18 and 60, as well as the leaders of the community were interned to camps of Targu-Jiu and Craiova.

From Darabani (Dorohoi county) the entire Jewish community, old people, women, children, even the disabled (about 2,000 people) were interned to camps of Oltenia (men to Targu-Jiu, women to Calafat).

From Siveni, Mihuleni, Ridiuti (Dorohoi county) the entire Jewish community (about 4,000 people) were evacuated; some men to the camp of Tirgu-Jiu, the other men, women and children to Dorohoi.

June 30, 1941

The Ministry of Interior orders to acquire Jewish hostages from each town in Moldova and Bucovina. They are to be shot dead in case of rebellion or terrorist acts. He also orders the internment of Jewish men from Jewish districts, mostly to schools or bigger buildings; guards are ordered next to them to punish them if they attempt to cause disturbances.

There was a curfew for Jews between 20.00 and 7.00 hours. /.../

In certain places (Dorohoi, Radauti) military authorities order Jews to wear a yellow star. /.../

July 3, 1941

Mihai Antonescu, Deputy President of the Council of Ministers, holds a secret meeting with the administrative clerks and military judges who are to be sent to Bessarabia and Bucovina. In the directives and rules issued this time, great emphasis is put on the strict and implacable attitude the authorities must display against Jews in these territories. Later all these were published in a leaflet, with the remarkable chapter called Ethnic and Political Cleansing. The directives urge for wild pogroms, and also contain concrete actions to be taken; internments to ghettos and deportations beyond the Dniester could be considered as the latter.

July 3, 1941

The attacks commence in the entire Romanian section of the front, from Ceremus to the Danube. At the same time starts the robbery of Jewish wealth, and the ghastly massacring of Jews wherever the Romanian army moves forward. Those who survive the massacres are collected in local, temporary camps.   /.../

July 5, 1941

The camp in Storojinetis divided into two parts: women and children are locked into the building of the elementary school, men into the orphanage which is two kilomentres away from the town; food is not provided, there is no medical service. /.../

July 18, 194

During a meeting of the Council of Ministers, Ion Antonescu arouses for hatred and announces his intention to have all Jews from Bessarabia and Bucovina to be deported.

July 8, 1941

Colonel Meculescu, Commander of the Gendarmerie Inspectorate in Kishinev, orders—among other things—the identification and arrest every Jew in the villages of Bessarabia, irrespective of their sex and age.

July 10, 1941

The Jewish marching column of Banila arrives to Storojinet. Their number is swollen up by Jews from the villages they passed through (Iadova, Berhomet, Panca, Cires). In Storojinet a camp is created in the synagogue, where 2,500 people are crowded. The guards torture their victims all the time, especially Lieutenant-Colonel Alexandrescu, Commander of the Draft (Recruiting) Centre, who beats Jews with his own hands, and rouses the citizens for looting and murder. He also forces people to work hard, although they have nothing else to eat but grass because he forbids them to leave the camp to get some food. /.../

July 18, 1941

The Highest Military Judge of the army goes for a supervising tour in Balti county. In this county, where 31,965 Jews had been indicated by the latest national census, and where their number must have been increased by natural population growth and the migrations of 1940, at the time of the control, there are not more than 3,481 Jews in three camps. Supposedly, there are 5,000 more of them in the county.

July 20, 1941

The Jews from Storojinet, who had been locked into the school and the orphanage, are collected into a ghetto consisting of two streets. The houses there had been completely robbed. Strict measures are introduced in the ghetto. Jews are obliged to wear a yellow star and there is a curfew at 1900 hours. They can provide themselves with food only after 10.00 hours. /.../

July 24, 1941

Jews taken from villages of Northern-Bucovina (Briceni, Chelminet, Babin, Trinca, Carjauti, Ianeuti etc.)—approximately 25,000 people—are collected in Coslar, and then are driven across the Dniester.

July 24, 1941

Jews who survived the massacres in Kishinev—approx. 11,000 people—are driven out of their homes, to a square which is surrounded by soldiers holding machine guns ready to shoot. Jews are mocked and pestered all day. In the evening they are allowed to occupy the houses on the southern side of the square. The ghetto is locked, guarded so as no one can leave it. /.../

July 27, 1941

The ghetto in Kishinev is limited to a few streets; they are in a district ruined by the bombardment so no house remained intact. Most of them do not have doors or windows. The latest national census in Kishinev indicated 50,603 Jews. Their number must have been increased by natural population growth and the migrations of 1940, at least as much as it was decreased by the escapes in the first days of the war. Yet, by this time there are only 10,311 left.

In each room there are 25-30-40 people crowded together. They are not allowed to leave the ghetto even to get some food. They are the targets of abuse of soldiers and guards. It is especially the officers who insult them, for whom visiting the ghetto is the funniest thing.   /.../

August 1, 1941

The Jews who survived the massacre in Hotin are driven towards east. The escorting soldiers and paramilitaries torture them on the way; in Romancauti they order a resting time so as to rape girls and women. /.../

August 2, 1941

Bessarabian Jews, who had been taken across the Dniester or scattered about in the Ukraine, were collected again in Moghilau. From there they are sent to Scazinet.

Approx. 4,000 are missing from the 25,000 people taken across the Dniester; they were killed by hunger, misery and the bullets of soldiers. /.../

August 6, 1941

Jews from Bessarabia and Bucovina are collected in Atachi, on the bank of the Dniester. First Jews from Noua Sulita and Storojinet arrive there. In the river, at the right bank of which they are taking a rest, more and more corpses of Jews are drifted by on the water. The Germans do not allow them to enter the Ukraine, therefore the Jews are forced back to Secureni. /.../

August 19, 1941

It is announced that the area between the Dniester and Bug (Transnistria) falls under Romanian administration, except for Odessa and its surroundings. At this time the Soviet troops are still in Odessa and will keep it for the next two months.

Teacher Gh. Alexianu is appointed governor of Transnistria.

August 19, 1941

The first news of the terrible misery of Bessarabian and Bucovinian Jews living in camps of Secureni and Edineti, arrive in Bucharest. The Union of the Jewish Community would like to aid them, but all their attempts fail. Their request handed in the Ministry of Interior is refused saying that only the Presidium of the State Council can decide in this issue. When their request is handed in there, too, they are given no reply. The General Headquarters replies very indecisively to their second request, without providing for a solution. /.../

August 30, 1941

Colonel Al. Rioasnu, governor of Bucovina died due to an unsuccessful (medical) operation in Chernovitz. He had been in office for only six months. During this time obediently but at the same time thoughtfully carried out Antonescu's orders. The massacres in Bucovina had been organized before his appointment. General Corneliu Calotescu was appointed to be his successor.

August 31, 1941

The setting up of Jewish camps in Bessarabia has been completed. There are 8,941 Jews in the three camps in Balti county, and 22,969 in Vertujeni, Soroca county. Although no official reports mention it, there might be approx. 10,000 Jews more in the same county, in Marculesti.

September 1, 1941

In Hotin county, which administratively belongs to the Governorship of Bucovina, there are 12,248 Jews in the camp of Edineti, and 10,201 in the camp of Secureni.   /.../

September 2, 1941

General Ion Topor, Highest Military Tribunal of the army, orders the Gendarmerie Inspectorate of Transnistria to start preparations to the deportation of Jews in the camps, to beyond the Dniester. The deportation starts on September 6, and the Jews will be taken in groups of 1,000 through the crossing-places of Criuleni-Karantin and Rezina-Rabnita. /.../

September 5, 1941

The 2nd Territorial Headquarters orders the Union of the Jewish Community to collect and hand over to the military authorities 5,000 complete civilian clothing (suits, overcoats, shoes, hats, shirts, underwear, socks); these will be given to Jews in camps and ghettos of Bessarabia.

Note: Although the command was entirely fulfilled, even over-fulfilled, due to a special rule announced later, the naked and barefoot Jews of Bessarabia and Transnistria did not get any of them.

September 11, 1941

The circumstances in the three big Bessarabian Jewish camps (Secureni, Edineti, Vertujeni) are appalling.

In Edineti, more than 12,000 people are located in five streets, 2,500 people in 26 peasant houses. Most of the interned Jews were from around Storojinet, which they left with a sack on the back, and what they had brought was either used up by themselves during the several weeks of the transportation, or were taken away. They were not able to pay 10 lei for a loaf of bread; all they bread got stale in the warehouse of the camp, but they were not given to the starving people. Most of the Jews were barefoot. Many of them almost naked. Some wrapped themselves into newspaper or brown paper. Although all were exhausted by the long journey, hunger and misery, they were forced to work. The guards, gendarmes and paramilitaries were mocking them while they were working.   /.../

The most terrible camp is located in Vertujeni. Here Colonel Agapie and Captains Buradescu and Radulescu are the lords. More than 20,000 people are crowded in a place which would not be enough for one tenth of them. There is no roof on most of the houses, because the tin was removed by the order of Colonel Agapie to make holders for lard and soap. The Jews were fatigued by the two months of wandering on both sides of the Dniester. They have nothing to be sold because everything was taken away from them on the way or in the camp. Despite their poverty, they have to pay 2 lei for each person who leaves the camp to get some food for them. They can hardly obtain water because they have to queue for hours at the few wells of the camp. They have to do hard and useless jobs, for instance pave the camp with stones brought from the Dniester, while starving, tortured, and beaten. Captains Buradescu and Radulescu, monsters of the camp, rape Jewish girls and women. Several dozens of people die every day due to misery, starvation, thirst and pains suffered.   /.../

September 20, 1941

Typhoid breaks out in the camp of Edineti. The commander of the camp threatens to shoot every Jew dead if the epidemic spreads on.   /.../

October 20, 1941

From the beginning of the month the camp of Marculesti acts as a collecting camp for those Jewish deportee groups which are to be taken across the Dniester at the crossing place of Rezina. In fact the camp in Marculesti was created for the purpose of looting and torturing.

Both looting and torture were directed by Colonel Vasile Agapie, commander of the camp, whose helpers were Captains Buradescu and Radulescu as well as Ion Mihailescu, a supervisor of the National Bank, who was sent there to exchange the rubles into lei, and to pay cash for the valuables. All of them walked in the camp equipped with sticks and pistols, and tortured everybody who they met, men, women, old people, the sick etc. Many people were beaten up by them so much that they died a few days later. Their subordinates and the gendarmes acted in the same fashion, beating their victims with anger similar to that of their commanders.

The Jews were deprived of all they rescued from the previous hell with the pretext of duty payment and foreign exchange. Everything was stolen around their hands: pieces of clothes, underwear, money (lei and foreign cash) jewelry (rings were pulled off the fingers by wringing them, earrings were torn out of the ears along with pieces of flesh), pillows and covers, cutlery, and even baby prams. Documents and identity cards of the deportees were confiscated and torn.   /.../

Due to starvation, misery and beating an enormous number of people died in the camp, where corpses were lying everywhere: in cellars, ditches, yards etc.

Every day a marching column of 2-3,000 people were set off from the camp to cross the Dniester at Rezina.

October 31, 1941

The deportation of Jews from the ghetto of Kishinev continued during the whole month. In rain, then in the early coming wintry weather, a marching column of 700 -1,000 was started almost every day on the highway of Orhei. The deportees were mocked and beaten by the gendarmes all the way. Sometimes the marching columns were stopped so that the gendarmes or the peasants could rob the Jews. The peasants got into the habit of hiding in the corn-fields to wait for the prisoner-transports to attack and rob them. Those who lagged behind out of exhaustion, were shot dead. /.../

There was constant terror, panic and hopelessness in the ghetto. Several people went mad, others committed suicide. The rest tried to insist on staying alive at any cost. /.../

November 8, 1941

The deportation of Jews from the camps of Vertujeni, Secureni and Edineti had ended. All survivors were taken across the Dniester, most of them were scattered near Atachi, in Moghilau county.

The deportations from the camp in Marculesti continue. After they cross the Dniester near Rabnita, the deportees are driven towards the Bug, to Balta and Tulcin counties.

November 20, 1941

The deportation from Marculesti of Jews collected from the camps of Bessarabia has come to an end. Only a few trains still come from Bucovina. It is requested that trains should not be directed to Marculesti any longer.

Deportations from Bucovina, Dorohoi County and the Chernovitz Ghetto

The Chronological Order of Events

October 8, 1941 - November 15, 1941

October 8, 1941

It was irrevocably decided that Jews from Bessarabia and Bucovina were to be deported; this had already been proposed in the first days of the war, as a means of "ethnic and political cleansing". Certain military organs had requested this as an action to be taken for the sake of the safety of the area directly behind the front line.

It was also definitely decided that Jewish deportees should be deprived of all their valuables.

This issue is not of great significance in Bessarabia any more, because more than half of the Jewish community was exterminated in the first two months of the war, and almost every survivor deported in September. There, only the remaining, approx. 10,000 Jews, who had been locked into the ghetto of Kishinev, were affected by these new measures. By this time all Jews in Northern-Bucovina had been either massacred or deported, except for the approx. 2,000 in Storojinet, and the 40 - 45,000 who had survived the massacres in Chernovitz.

In Southern-Bucovina a great number of Jews were murdered in the summer of 1940 and in July, 1941. Some of the Jews were evacuated from here in the first few days of the war, but were later brought back. However, no one was taken across the frontier. (...) According to the figures of the last official national census, the local Jewish community amounted to 23,844 people. /.../

October 9, 1941

In Southern-Bucovina the deportation of Jews starts simultaneously in every village.

At dawn it is made known to the public by spoken order, by town-criers and by the posting of notices that all Jews must leave the place in the shortest time possible (in Suceava within 8 hours, and in Itcani within 4), and everyone is allowed to bring with them as much as they can carry. /.../

October 10, 1941

Measures are ordered to be taken for the organization of the ghetto in Chernovitz, and for the deportation of all Jews from the area of Northern-Bucovina.

Firstly, on October 11, the entire Jewish community of Chernovitz is ghettoized.

From the ghetto they are gradually transported to the first indicated stations (two trains of fifty boxcars depart daily).

From this day forth, all Jewish property becomes of the property of the state.

The task of collecting all the Jews, guarding the ghetto, loading them onto the train and guarding it, is the responsibility of the Military Headquarters of Bucovina, and the Gendarme Inspectorate of Chernovitz. Their number has been increased by a battalion directed there to help in the execution of these tasks. /.../

October 11, 1941

The Jews of Chernovitz are ghettoized with special care.

It is impossible to imagine a picture more heartbreaking than that of Chernovitz on that day. During an eight hour period, approx. 50,000 people of varying ages, of different social and intellectual strata, who had lived scattered in the town, are now moving silently in one direction, leaving their homes, carrying on their backs and in their hands or pulling in barrows all that remains of the property of an entire generation (or in many cases several generations) had gathered. /.../

The ghetto was so small that people could live there only among the worst conditions. The luckiest settled down in houses, 30-40 per room. Those who arrived later found shelter for themselves in attics, cellars or stables. The last to arrive could not get more than the gutters in the yards and streets.

Movement was not restricted within the ghetto, but once a Jew entered it, he needed special permission from the Governor of Bucovina to walk out. It was very difficult to get such permission, for example, to take out corpses and bury them in the Jewish cemetery which was not in the vicinity of the ghetto.

October 11, 1941

The President of the Union of Jewish Religious Communities turned to Marshal Antonescu with his second request, asking him not to allow this mortal tragedy to happen, whose participants are made to start a long journey naked, without food and without the chance of acquiring it, in rain, cold and snow. /.../

October 12, 1941

One train carrying Jews from Southern-Bucovina is stopped on free track 50 kilometres from Radauti. The Gendarmes order those in charge of the freight-cars chosen from among Jews to tell everybody that they must hand over all the gold and other valuables, as well as the keys to their abandoned homes. It is announced that they will be thoroughly searched in Marculesti, and those who hiding anything, will be shot dead. An entire suitcase of gold and jewelry is collected. /.../

<h1 style="text-align:center">October 19, 1941</h1>

Marshal Antonescu, the Leader of the State, replies in a letter to Dr. W. Filderman, President of the Union of Jewish Religious Communities for the two petitions he submitted on the issue of deportation campaigns from Bessarabia and Bucovina.

The letter is obviously of political character. The deportation is presented as a deserved action for all that the citizens had committed there in 1940, during the withdrawal of the Romanian army, and under Soviet rule. He attempts to justify the measures with the atrocities committed by Soviet-Jewish commissars at the front. /.../

The letter, dated October 19, and received on October 20, also appeared in the newspapers on October 27, 1941, serving as an excuse for an organized ghastly and base press campaign. War-time anti-Semitic hatred reached its psychological peak at this time. The publication of the letter and the press campaign took place after the terrible explosion in Odessa, when a great number of Romanian high-ranking officers were killed due to carelessness.

Not a single line was written about the explosion. Still, it became known through the public and rumurs started to be whispered. The Marshal's letter and the anti-Semitic campaign were used to deceive the public. /.../

<h1 style="text-align:center">October 27, 1941</h1>

The marching column of Jews collected from the surroundings of Chernovitz arrives in the forest of Cosauti, where they discover hundreds of Jewish corpses lying on the ground everywhere. The Gendarmes are robbing their victims with increasingly more barbaric means. On the road from Marculesti towards the Dniester, several Jews are taken out of the marching columns, and sold to peasants. The price is between 1,500-2,000 lei depending on the quality of the victim's clothing. After the Gendarme received the money, he shot the Jew, and gave the corpse to the peasant so that he could pull the clothes off it. After marching for two days the columns crossed the Dniester near Iampol on a narrow bridge while being beaten with clubs and rifle butts. Those who lost their balance, fell into the water; they were left to drown.

November 10, 1941

The first marching columns organized from deportees from Dorohoi arrive in Atachi; approx. 3,000 people. Before being driven across the Dniester, they are held back for 24 hours in the cold and rain, and guarded by frontier guards. Other soldiers search them, depriving these poor people of their last valuables.

November 15, 1941

The deportation of Jews from Chernovitz ended. By this time approximately 30,000 Jews had been deported from the town, and the 15,600 who remained had received permission to do so from the selection committee, as had the 4,000 who were given temporary exemption permits by the Town Mayor.

December 6, 1941

Ion Antonescu is not satisfied with the activity of the President of the Union of Jewish Religious Communities, since due to this, he had to cancel the deportation of 20,000 Jews from Chernovitz. He decides to remove him from as head of the Jewish Religious Community, and disbands all Jewish community organizations. In their place, he sets up the Jewish Central Office, based on the German model created in the countries they occupied.

December, 1941

The last marching columns of Jews from Bucovina and Dorohoi county cross the Dniester near Atachi. The first period of the deportation of Romanian Jews has ended.

Murders in Odessa and in the Counties of Berezovca and Golta

The Chronological Order of Events

October 16, 1941 - December 1942

October 16, 1941

Romanian and German troops occupy Odessa, from where the Red Army had withdrawn a few days before. Although the occupiers do not meet with any resistance, they murder a great number of citizens, mostly Jews.

October 22, 1941

A time bomb explodes in the building of the Romanian Headquarters. The explosion kills 16 officers, 35 soldiers, 9 non-commissioned officers, civilian employees and Commander Gl. Glogojeanu himself. Three hours later, Gl. C. Trestioreanu, Commander of the 13th Infantry Regiment, who automatically stepped into the place of the Commander of Town, reports the following to the 4th Army: "I have taken measures for the Jews and communists to be hanged in the public places of Odessa".

October 23, 1941

The so-called revenge actions have started. By morning there are gallows standing everywhere, with victims hanging on them. People are shot dead randomly in every part of the city. At noon, the executions stop; so far approx. 5,000 people have been killed, most of them are Jews.

October 23, 1941

Ion Antonescu orders the execution of 200 communists for each murdered Romanian or German officer, and 100 for ordinary soldiers. He also orders the taking of communist and Jewish hostages...

October 24, 1941

Some of the people collected by the police and the army, were taken to the edge of Odessa, next to the town gate in Dalnic by the 2nd Squadron of the 10th Machine Gun Battalion. The road, three kilometres long was lined with the corpses of women, children and the disabled. They were shot dead because they could not keep up with the marching columns. The first 40-50 people to arrive at the execution Site were tied up, made to lie face down in an anti-tank ditch. Then a few soldiers, led by Lieutenant-Colonel Nicolae Deleanu, shot them dead.

This was followed by mass executions. The victims were taken into four warehouses, on the walls of which holes were cut for machine guns. Lieutenant-Colonels Deleanu and Coca D. Niculescu order fire to be opened on the unfortunate people.

At dusk, at approx. 17.00 hrs, they set the warehouses ablaze. While the victims burn in the flames, the soldiers continue to shoot them with machine guns, and the officers throw hand-grenades at them.

October 25, 1941

At 17.35 hrs, exactly 48 hours after the explosion, they blow up one of the warehouses, which still included the wounded.

October, 1941

A number of Jews who survived the massacres in Odessa, as well as those who are collected in the southern counties of Transnistria (Oceacov, Berezovca, Golta), are locked up in camps called ghettos. They are treated terribly. In the ghetto people die everyday of starvation, disease and misery. /.../

November 11, 1941

Gh. Alexian, Governor of Transnistria, issues Directive No. 23, which regulates the daily routine of the Jewish citizens of Transnistria.

Jews are allowed to live only in certain places, assigned to them by the Gendarme Inspectorate. They are registered separately, farms are organized for them, and they are used for agricultural labor, roads and bridge repair work, lumber-jacking and carrying stones or other materials. The workers are given daily food coupons; day-laborers 1 RKKS Mark, and skilled workers 2 RKK Marks. /.../

Those who leave the place assigned to them, are declared spies, and military laws valid during war-time are used against them.

November 20, 1941

Colonel E. Brosteanu, Commander of the Gendarme Inspectorate of Transnistria, is worried that Transnistria is, "filling up with communists and Jews", who might commit hostile acts later. He, therefore, asks for commands from the Gendarme Central Inspectorate, saying: "only the extermination of criminals and fanatic communists will free mankind from the threat of communism".

Under directive No.23, most of the Jews are removed from their dwelling places. In the northern part of the territory, in Moghilev 3,733; in Sargorod approx. 2,000; in Rabnita 1,467; in Tulcin 118 (the other 3,005 are sent to the camp in Peciora); in Spikov, 27 (the other 848 are locked up in Rogozna)—these are the remaining Jews.

In the southern part of Transnistria almost all local Jews are interned in camps in Golta county; in Bogdanovca there are 48,000 Jews; in Dumanovca, 18,000; in Acmicetca, 4,000. In these camps deportees, are deprived of everything they own (gold and jewelry were the most sought after). They were subjected to the most terrible forms of torture; starvation and misery were the most lethal methods.

During this time there was an unidentified number of Jews in Balti (a few thousand, perhaps), and in Odessa approximately 30,000. /.../

December 21, 1941

With the help of Lieutenant-Colonel Modest Isopescu , Prefect of Golta county, the extermination of Jews in the camp of Bogdanovca is started. The first victims are chosen from among the sick and crippled. They are locked up in stables, which are filled with straw, then petrol is poured on before they are set ablaze. While the stables are burning with the people locked inside them, they take the other interned people, (approx. 43,000) to the nearby forest in groups of 3-400, where they are killed with exploding bullets. The massacre continues on December 21, 22 and 23; it is stopped at Christmas time and restarted on December 28, and finished on December 29.

The corpses are put together in piles 4 - 5 metres long and 2 metres high so that they can be cremated. This terrible act is carried out by a group of 200 Jews for 2 months. Having finished with this work, 150 of them are shot dead.

January 10, 1942

The Governor of Transnistria issued directive No.7, according to which all Jews in Transnistria are to submit their gold, jewelry and valuables, and must present themselves for internment in the ghetto of Slobotka. /.../

January 11, 1942

The deportation of Jews started from the ghetto in Odessa to the Berezovca-Vasilievo region. On the first day 856 Jews were deported, mostly old people, women and children. On -

    January 13:   986
    January 14:   1,201
    January 15:   1,091

people, most of them between the ages of 50 and 80.

By then more than 6,000 Jews had been deported from Odessa. The pains suffered en route were terrible. On -

January 17: 1,104
January 18: 1,293
January 19: 1,010
January 20:   926 were deported.

January 21, 1942

As all train transportation ceases, the deportation of Jews is also stopped. The Gendarme Inspectorate reports that they cannot accommodate the evacuees; they are brought to the stables of kholhoz (co-operative farms). The temperature is -20 Celsius, [4 F. below zero] due to this, starvation and old age, many collapse and freeze along the roads. The dead bodies are buried in anti-tank ditches.

January 22, 1942

The deportation of Jews from ghettos in Odessa continues, 1,807 Jews, mostly old people, women and children are sent to Berezovca. /.../ On -

January 23: 1,396
January 24: 2,000
January 31, 1942

The deportation continues, 1,200 Jews are taken away on -

February 1: 2,256. /.../

The extermination of Jews from Golta county has ended, the 22,000 Jews in the camps of Dumanovca and Acmicetca are massacred.

March 9, 1942

The Jews transported from Odessa to the region of Berezovca-Mostovoi-Vasilievo, after having been looted and tortured, are handed over to the Germans. When they arrive there, their extermination is started. /.../

December, 1942

The suffering of Jews who once lived in Odessa and in the southern counties of Transnistria has ended. Their complete extermination has been accomplished. The statistical figures of the Romanian Central Jewish Office show (after a delegation of the Aid Committee examined the whole territory from Odessa to Moghilev) that in the southern part of Transnistria there are only 60 Jews living in Odessa and 425 in Berezovca county. A total of 485 people...

Deportations in the Spring and Autumn of 1942

The Chronological Order of Events

June 7, 1942 - October 13, 1942

June 7, 1942

Due to initiatives so far unknown, an order of General Corneliu Calotescu, Governor of Bucovina, and under the direct control of Major Stere Marinescu, Head of Cabinet, a new group of Jews was deported from among those who were still in Chernovitz. It seems that this plan was aimed at the deportation of those 4,000 Jews who, during the deportation of November, 1941 had been selected to for permission to stay in the town from Dr. Traian Popovici, ex-town mayor who had fallen out of favor by then. /.../

Some of the lists of names were compiled in April at the Governor's office, and two days before the deportation, the county branch of the Romanian Central Jewish Office was asked to urgently provide the list of the Jews who remained in the town under the Popovici permit.

The Jewish organizations (both in Bucharest and in Chernovitz) received this information in time, but all of their attempts to prevent this disaster were in vain. Leading Romanian authorities, intoxicated by their illusory military successes, remained deaf throughout the summer of 1942. The clerks were only paying attention and holding out their palms to make a profit from the misfortune of the Jews. Stere Marinescu, for example, received 500,000 lei as monthly allowance from the Jews before the deportation. This, however, did not prevent him from accomplishing the deportation with cruelty and barbarity.

Under his order, patrols of policemen and soldiers joined by representatives of the Town Hall, in the middle of the night, went to the Jewish homes selected according to the prepared lists, and collected approx. 1,000 people, men, women and children, and did not allow them to bring more with them than what they could carry on their backs. /..../

Among the people collected there were a number of Polish citizens who held Chilean passport. Also 66 in-patients from the lunatic asylum were forced to leave, along with the hospital staff, although the latter had residence permits signed by the Governor himself. /..../

Directly after the deportation, the homes of Jews remained empty. Signs prepared in advance were stuck onto the doors which said that the goods inside had became the property of Town Hall. Later they were divided among those Romanians who laid claim to them; they were given to those hyenas from all social and intellectual strata, who flooded the town in the hope of getting rich. The furniture remained in their hands for a year, when under formal sales contracts it became their property forever.

June 14, 1942

The second transportation of Jews was collected and sent to Transnistria in the same barbaric manner as the first, with looting and torture. Those living at the old people's home (with people over the age of 80), as well as hospital patients wearing only hospital gowns were taken out of their beds were also included in this transportation. The doctor on duty protested against the taking of patients1 and was subsequently arrested.

June 14, 1942

Under the order of the Governor of Bucovina, 450 Jews are deported from Dorohoi. Most are men, breadwinners, who had been in labor service in November 1941, when the first deportation separated them from their wives and children. When they returned from labor service, they found their flats sealed, their families taken away and their property confiscated. They did not even receive permission to remain in the town. If some of them still managed to sneak into the city, patrols surrounded the streets, collected them and took them directly to the railway station.

June 28, 1942

A new Black Sunday for the Jews of Chernovitz. Another Jewish group of about 2,000 is deported. The people are collected at night and at dawn under the same barbaric circumstances as on the two previous Sundays (June 7 and 14). They were taken to the sports grounds in Makabi where they were the targets of mockery all day. The operations were once again directed by Major Stere Marinescu. His helpers were Police Commander Traian Ionescu and Manea Bocioaga, who was the co-ordinating officer of Jewish issues in the governorship. Before that time, the latter person had been the financial executive of the governorship. On this occasion, people who had been given permission to stay by the governor were officially deprived of it. /..../

In the evening, before the train departed, Major Marinescu checked the freight-cars. Since he realized that there was still room in them, at about 19.00 hrs he gave an order to collect Jews from a few streets of the Rosa district. The freight-cars were still not completely full, therefore Marinescu gave another order in the middle of the night, according to which, all Jews living in Pitei Street were to be collected. There were people among them who had been given permission to stay only a few hours previously by the selection committee. /.../

August 8, 1942

Since German troops arrived in the country, the German embassy attempted for the first time to actively influence the Romanian government and the general public in order to exterminate the Romanian Jewish population. Everything so far had taken place exclusively on Romanian initiatives, and was carried out exclusively by Romanian authorities. It is natural that the pursuits and crimes they ordered or allowed to happen, were mostly the passive consequences of the influential Nazi mentality. However, Romania was not forced to do anything by the Germans, except for the demolishing traditional Jewish communities and substituting them with the Jewish Office. There were no ratified obligations to prescribe the persecution and execution of Jews. The occurrences were the consequences of the fact that Romania had joined the Berlin-Rome Axis.

The relatively favorable situation at the front—the German-Hungarian forces were standing in front of Voroniezh, the German-Romanian troops were approaching Stalingrad as well as Krasnodar and Majkop—induced the Gestapo to start its actions planned a long time ago, whose aim was the complete extermination of Romanian Jews. These actions had already been started earlier in territories occupied by the Germans.

In the official journal of the German Embassy of Bucharest, the *Bukarester Tageblatt,* an article appears with the title "Rumanien wird judenrein" (Romania will be cleared of Jews), which gives a full account of the plan to deport the entire Romanian Jewish population. The action will be started in the autumn, and must be accomplished by the following autumn.

A similar article—which seems to have been written by the same person—appears in the same day in the *Donauzeitung,* the official newspaper of the Gestapo in the Balkans, published in Belgrade. Two days later the *Volkisher Beobachter* publishes the news, too. It is of significance that the Romanian press remains silent on the issue. /..../

Some days later (August 13) Radu Lecca, Commissioner of Jewish Issues, is called to Berlin to participate in the conference of the SD (Sicherheitsdienst) with Gustaw Richter, Head of the Jewish Department of the Romanian Gestapo.

The content and decisions of the meeting are unknown but can be deducted, since a month later (on September 26-28) German Railways held another meeting in Berlin.

In the absence of the delegation of Romanian Railways (although invited, they excused themselves by requesting the postponement of the meeting) a decision was made to collect the entire Romanian Jewish population in Adjud county, from where every second day a transportation of 2,000 people was to be started to the death-camp of Belzen in Poland.

August 15, 1942

For some weeks, the Jewish population feel even more threatened than usual. The news of further groups of Jewish deportees from Chernovitz, cause not only pain, but also fear. The latest announcements of the military and civilian authorities (General Command and the Ministry of the Interior), with their stereotyped and hurtful refrains ("they will be deported to Transnistria along with their families"), and news published in the German press—to test public reaction, which arrogantly spread the rumor about the deportation of the entire Romanian-Jewish population, caused general panic. /.../

The recently leaked news is indeed horrifying. It was learnt simultaneously in Bucharest (from Radu Lecca, government representative of Jewish affairs) and Timisoara (from authenticated local resources):the decision had been made for the deportation of Jews from the major towns of Transylvania and Banat, i.e. from towns close to the Romanian-Hungarian border: Timisoara, Arad, Beius, Turda, Sighisoara, Brasov.

The leaders of the threatened communities (Dr. S. Ligeti and I. Tenner from Timisoara, Aladar Lakatos from Arad, A. Fellter from Sibiu, etc.) gather in Bucharest to commence activity. They are not supported by the Romanian Central Jewish Office, but receive assistance from the underground leadership of the Jews. They do everything in their power to hand in requests backed up by documents to all leading forums.

The first benevolent action was taken by doctor Stroescu, family physician of Antonescu and Director of the newly established Palace of War-Invalids, for which he tried to beg Jewish money by all means. He starts an action with great enthusiasm in the interest of Jews, although the condition of this is an amount of 100 million lei collected by Jews from Transylvania and Banat for the Palace of War-Invalids.

At the same time they gained the support of His Holiness Balan, the Metropolitan of Transylvania. The old High Priest traveled from Paltinis to Bucharest just for this reason. His Samaritan action was supported fully by Her Majesty Elena, the Queen Mother. It is said that this dramatic issue was decided in the royal palace over lunch, to which Balan His Holiness, the Metropolitan, Ion Antonescu and the Queen were invited, and where Her Majesty supported with dignity and extreme firmness the cause of those persecuted.

They also received the active support of His Excellency Monsignor Andrea Cassulo, Papal Nuncio, and His Excellency Rene de Weck, Ambassador of Switzerland, who did not hesitate to lend the support resolutely and unambiguously.

It will always be a secret, which of these actions was the crucial one. So far not even the decision is known with which Antonescu modified the murderous decision. However, the fact is that the leaders of the Jewish communities were informed, (even if not concretely and finally) that the idea of deporting of Jews from Transylvania and Banat was abandoned. /.../

September 13, 1942

On the occasion of the Jewish New Year, Cordel Hull, the American Secretary of State, turned to Jews living in every part of the world with a moving speech, in which he placed emphasis on the solidarity of the American and Jewish nations.

Romanian public opinion was strongly influenced by the speech, which caused strange reactions.

The Romanian press, for instance, commented on the speech with a certain sense of respect. Even the blackmailing gutter newspaper, *Porunca Vremii,* abandoned its aggressive and vulgar tone temporarily. The Editor-in-Chief of the paper, I. P. Prudeni, writes this under the title "The Meaning of a Speech" in the issue of September 15, 1942:

"Our aggravated hatred is mixed with the reserved admiration we feel in seeing the stubborn will to believe, calculated resignation and the special strength of bearing suffering and persecution. The basic virtue of the Jews lies in the unusual strength with which they manage to land on their feet after each disaster. This is what the issue looks like after removing the vulgar insults from among the hostility which never solves anything."

One ex-minister of Antonescu's strongly refuses to be a member of the government again. He gives the following reason to his friends: "Haven't you read Cordel Hull's speech? Why should I fight the Jews right now?"

The Minister of the Interior, General Dumitru Popescu, calls to Dr. W. Filderman for an audience, who he had not met for more than a year since he was dismissed from the leadership of the community. The General literally told him this: "Although you are not the legal leader of the Jews, I must turn to you with my request. You must remember my announcements which were repeated many times, that I do not agree with what is being done against the Jews. But my power is restricted to as far as the Prut. Therefore, it is not in my power to do anything now. The deportation campaigns are in General Vasiliu's hands, who—it seems—has made an agreement with the Germans. Please, tell the Jews not to hand in requests to me in which they ask me to exempt them from deportation or to give them time since I cannot help them in any way

The audience lasted a long time, and was repeated the following day on the minister's request. He showed a keen interest in the details of Jewish issues and expressed his indignation at what was happening to the Jews. He did not forget to disassociate himself from the persecution of Jews, which were initiated and carried out by the government, of which he was a member. He again asked Dr. Filderman to pass the aforementioned request to the Jews.

However, on exactly the same day the Minister of the Interior had said these things (September 22, 1942, on the day of Yom Kippur), while he was getting rid of the responsibility of past and present, the organs led by him did the following:

1.   The Central Police Station of the Capital sent 148 Jews to Transnistna (with their families), who were accused of having avoided labor service.

2.   Policemen and police officers, on behalf of the National Centre of Romanianization, removed the old people from the Elisabet old people's home, which became the property of the above-mentioned organization.

3.   The Gendarmes of Mostovoi (Berezovca county) helped the SS rob and kill 600 Jews, who had been brought there from the Old Kingdom and Transylvania two weeks before under the order of the Ministry of the Interior.

However, it is also true, that General Dumitru Popescu was a little more far-sighted than the Ministry of Propaganda, and people similar to him also started to compete to win certificates proving their good behavior. /.../

Life and Death in Transnistria

The Chronological Order of Events
October 1,1941 - March 20,1944

October 1, 1941

The first Romanian Jewish deportees to step onto Transnistrian soil were the most unfortunate. They were Bessarabian Jews, collected in August - survivors of the massacres. They were driven here and there on both sides of the Dniester first by the Romanian, then by the German army. They crossed Moghilau and were allowed to rest in Scazinet. After being tortured, robbed and starved, one third of them had perished before they arrived at the ghastly camp in Vertujeni. The first marching columns departed from there on September 16, to cross the river Dniester after two more weeks of suffering at two places: those driven towards Iampol crossed near Cosauti, others taken to Rabnita did the same near Rezina. The new marching columns, which were later driven towards the river Bug, were assembled at these two gates of Transnistria. The first marching column was allowed to rest in Barzula, then arrived in Grozdovca and stayed there. Throughout the entire journey they had to withstand the beating and jeering of non-commissioned officer Tarca, on whose orders several deportees were executed. Later, after they had rested, they found themselves in the hands of a corporal who considered himself the leader of the camp of Grozdovca. He counted them, while taking them over, hitting each one on the back with an iron bar.

The marching columns moved on different routes but all suffered an unfortunate fate. /.../

November 1, 1941

Throughout the month of October marching column followed marching column through the three crossing-points (Rabnita, Iampol and Moghilev). No one was allowed to stay at the first two. The deportees who were driven there, were forced to move on towards the Bug, where they were locked into the ghettos of Bersad, Obodovca, Tibulovca, Olgopol, Ustea, etc. They had to walk almost naked on the road sodden with the sticky mud of early winter. They suffered first from the greed and barbarity of their escorts. A great number were either murdered or died of cold, starvation or complete exhaustion. The corpses were not even buried, just left on the meadows where dogs and ravens finished what humans had started. Occasionally, risking execution, a mother dug out a handful of soil to bury a child who had died in her arms. When they arrived at their destination, the deportees could only find shelter in stables without doors and windows (frequently next to cattle) or in pigsties, barns, etc. One could see the terrible picture of completely exhausted people leaning against the walls of stables; they did not talk, moan, eat or curse, they simply waited in total senility until death forced them to collapse onto the floor or another dead body. It was at this time, in the autumn of 1941 that the expression "Totenwande" (death walls) came into being throughout Transnistria. This was the beginning of the ghettos at the bank of Bug.

The authorities in Moghilev did not want to allow Jews to stay there, either. Here, however, due to a number of coincidences, a few of those who had crossed the Dniester near Atachi had the opportunity to partly decide their own future. For others, however, this choice later turned out to be fatal.   Transnistria was entered here by Jews from Southern Bucovina, and a number of Jews from Chernovitz and Dorohoi also crossed the Dniester at this point. Some Jews were collected from their places of work, but others were rich people who were able to take their savings across the Dniester, in spite of organized robberies. As a result, they had enough money to buy a little goodwill. The first Jews deported from Suceava and Campulung bought transport vehicles and drove away, spreading themselves throughout the county. The first deportees continued their journey on German lorries. They paid 50-125,000 lei to the prefect, his deputy or the police superintendent, and became inhabitants of the ghettos in Sargorod, Copaigorod, Djurin, Murafa, Smerinca, etc. Only a few of these lucky ones were able to continue by lorry.

The poor people, who did not have enough money to pay the tremendous amount required for transportation, and those, who had money but could not find room on the lorries, started their journey on foot on the sodden roads in rain and snow. Their suffering was appalling, and for some also fatal. A number of Jews, the first to arrive from Suceava, were forced onwards on foot towards Lucinet, Copaigorod and Bar, to the north-western part of Transnistria on a road which was more like a swamp from one end to the other. At the point where this road crossed the main Moghilev - Ozarinet road, 28 people were unable to pull their feet out of the mud. They sank even further in their attempts to free themselves. No one was allowed to help them. Dr. Abraham Sapirer, a lawyer, objected to what was being done to the Jews, and tried to assist them, but the Gendarmes shot him dead. The marching columns passed by and could do no more than just watch them as they waited to die. All of them died. /.../

There were similar cases on other roads to Transnistria. Several hundred Jews drowned in swamps. /.../

November 30, 1941

The last marching columns from Chernovitz and Dorohoi crossed the Dniester. The authorities acknowledged the deportation of 118,000 people, half of whom crossed through Moghilev. Approx. 15,000 (25%) were able to stay in the town, but only one third of these received legal permission to do so, and had to pay a large sum for this right. Under orders from the County Head Office, existing permits were subject to validation, and no further permits were to be issued. /.. ./

December 1, 1941

Wherever Jewish deportees were accommodated, dysentery, typhoid fever and petechial typhus broke out on an epidemic scale. In Bershad there was an epidemic of typhus before the arrival of the first deportees. In Sargorod, the first cases of typhus appeared on October 16, a month after the first deportees arrived. At that time petechial typhus had not yet hit Moghilev, but an increasing number of people were displaying symptoms of typhoid fever. /.../

December 10, 1941

Five months after hundreds of thousands of people had been hunted out of their homes, and two months after the actual start of the deportation campaign, after tens of thousands of people had died of starvation and disease, and following the spread of fatal epidemics, which could not be contained due to lack of medicine, soap, paraffin, clothing, fuel, food, etc., the Presidium of the Council of Ministers decided to permit the Union of Jewish Religious Communities to send money and medicine to Jews deported to Transnistria.

This permission was the final manifestation of a connection between the Antonescu Government and the traditional Jewish organization. Six days later, it was disbanded, and replaced with a Jewish organization whose structure was based on German police patterns. The leadership of this new organ took over the task of assisting Jews who had been deported lo Transnistria, however, because of its reluctance to act and its servile manner, the organization could not be counted on.

Dr. N. Ghingold spokesperson and general secretary of the Romanian Central Jewish Office expressed his personal view that action aimed at aiding deportees should be stopped, because it is contrary to government policy, and since all deportees must be considered enemies of the home land, and Jews are to considered in the same way. He continued by saying that those who insisted on carrying out acts of humanitarian aid, by doing so would undertake serious personal obligations and risks. He claimed that his authority spread as far as the river Prut, but he could not interfere in issues beyond the Prut.

The Aid Committee, which had been established alongside the Union of Jewish Religious Communities in January 1941, immediately following the Iron Guard revolt, could not accept this stand. They dismissed the fears of the leader of the Central Jewish Office, and decided to undertake both the task itself and the responsibility. Making use of the fact that one of the most enthusiastic initiators of deportee-aid, Dr. M. Zimmer, a lawyer, was trusted by Mihai Antonescu, the committee attempted to find out the latter's opinion concerning the issue. Through the proposal of the Deputy Prime Minister, supported by the written acceptance of the real leaders of the Jews, Dr. Zimmer agreed to join the Central Jewish Office, and direct—along with A. Schwefelberg, lawyer, and Fred Saraga—actions aimed at assisting deportees.   /.../

January 5, 1942

In Obadovca the petechial typhus epidemic is devastating and cannot be contained. The whole camp is declared a quarantine zone, surrounded with barbed wire and guarded with weapons. The interned people are not allowed to leave the camp, even to get food. As a result, a large number die, because of the epidemic itself and of starvation.   /.../

January 20, 1942

In Tibulovca 180 people survived from the 2,000 interned in November (100 men, 76 women and 4 children); all of them have frostbite on their limbs. They were allowed to move into the village, but they had to give money or their remaining items of clothing.   /.../

January 31, 1942

The petechial typhus epidemic has broken out in every area in the northern part of Transnistria where deported Jews live. There are only a few places where this epidemic is unknown, because in these regions (Djurin, Murafa, Smerinca), accommodation conditions are slightly more humane. The epidemic spreads faster in densely populated areas, i.e. Bershad, Sargorod, Moghilev.   /.../

February 6, 1942

One hundred and sixty-five corpses were taken to the cemetery in Sargorod but could not be buried because the ground was frozen. A fire was lit in the -40 Celsius temperature [40 F below zero]. It burned for 24 hours. This was the only way the mass-grave could be dug. In Bershad corpses were lying about everywhere for 3 - 4 weeks because they could not be buried because of the frost and a lack of workers. There were cases when 200 corpses were collected one day. /.../

February 17, 1942

Throughout Transnistria, but primarily in small villages, Jews are at the mercy of every beast in any power position, however slight. In Obodovca, Stefanescu, an engineer at the Agricultural Centre, is the monster who haunts the deportees. Even though in his job he has no connection with Jews, he takes the wildest measures against them. He beats and tortures them, and uses barbed wire to prevent them from buying food, and at the same time, for exorbitant sums of money he arbitrarily issues permits entitling the holders to stay in Obodovca. /.../

March 31, 1942

The petechial typhus epidemic reaches its peak in all contaminated villages. /.../ Doctors, one after the other, become victims of their profession. In Moghilev, 25 doctors became ill as early as February, the chief physician included; of the 27 doctors in Sargorod 23 became ill, i. e. 85%, 12 died, 52% of the doctors. The undertaker is unable to finish his work. There are always 60-80 corpses awaiting burial in the cemetery in Moghilev. /.../

The highest numbers of fatalities from the epidemic are in areas along the bank of the Bug. The general misery, in which the deportees lived, did not help prevent the epidemic. It raged on until it faded away by itself. In Bershad and its surrounding villages, approx. 20,000 people died of petechial typhus. In Ustea alone, some 5 kms from the Bug, 1,600 died from among the 2,500 deportees. /.../

June 5, 1942

The petechial typhus epidemic, which had become less of a threat with the passing of spring, ceased almost completely. The survivors prepared for battle against ensuing dangers, and closed the chapter on the previous, tragic, winter.

In Moghilev 4,401 people were counted with typhus, 1,254 of these died, putting the death rate at 28%. However, this data is not accurate since not every patient was recorded. It is suggested, there were approx.7,000 patients in the town, approx. half of whom died.

Both the number of patients and deaths were much higher in the other places, where the death rate was more than 50%. In Bershad it was 85% as a consequence of housing conditions. We will never know the exact figures, because (at least in the first winter) no one dealt with the registration and burial of the dead. When people died, their corpses were collected from the houses or roadsides, and thrown into ditches. Others were left to decompose in meadows. It is supposed that in the winter of 1941-42, the epidemic killed 50% of the Jews who, having survived massacres, camps and transportation, crossed the Dniester in October and November of 1941. This supposition was justified by the report of General C.Z. Vasiliu, Deputy Secretary of State. It claims that 110,033 Jews were evacuated, and only 50,741 were alive in September 1943. The missing 59,392 were written off as victims of the epidemic.

June 10, 1942

The camp in Scazinet was created from the ruined barracks of what had once been a school for officers. It was composed of two parts built on either side of the main road. The buildings on the right—after haphazard renovation—were turned into living quarters. The structures on the left had no windows and doors; some buildings did not even have roofs; they were in fact stables, and people suffered in these for months in the most terrible chaos.

The buildings on the right housed deportees who had managed to save some of their money, or because of their good connections were able to receive aid in Moghilev. On the left side, however, hunger reigned. A number of those interned had no choice but to eat grass from the meadows and leaves from trees. There was also a lack of water, and thirst was usually more lethal than hunger. The deportees started to dig near the camp in an attempt to find water. They did not find any, but they did stumble across an anti tank ditch full of corpses; they found rags, sacks and documents, and the remains of those Bessarabian Jews who had been killed by the Germans in August 1941. /.../

June 16 1942

The County Head Office of Moghilev sent his guidelines concerning the setting up of ghettos to the Police Stations, Gendarme Legions and Mayor's Offices under its authority.

In the order enclosed with the guidelines Colonel Nasturas, County Head (Poiana Volbura, a poet) emphasized that the execution of this decree "is an issue of Romanian honor and dignity". /.../

June 30, 1942

Jews in Moghilev were enclosed in a ghetto confined to only a few streets. The 16,000 people were crowded together, and 20-30 shared each room. Since many of the buildings had been destroyed by flooding, hundreds of families were forced to sleep in the open air, next to walls unprotected by roofs.

Since their arrival in Transnistria, all Jews were forced to wear the star of David on the left side of their chests as a distinguishing sign. In places, where directives were carried out with particular strictness, they also had to wear the signs on their backs. This primarily affected those Jews who worked in open areas. In other places, such as Sargorod and Smerinca, houses were also marked with yellow stars. The sign had to be worn inside the ghetto as well up until the time of liberation. /.../

July 30, 1942

The number of children being sent into the orphanage in Moghilev was constantly increasing. When deportees were taken to Scazinet, many parents handed their children over to the orphanage so as to save them from certain death. On this day the number of children reached 450.

The health of children in the orphanage gradually worsened. They were infested with lice, barely dressed, and their feet were wrapped in rags. Their itching bodies were covered in skin diseases,which spread with each attack of itching, and they suffered from severe diarrhea. As a result of the harsh winter, most of them fell victim to severe frostbite, and the insides of their mouths became inflamed.

August 1, 1942

Since their arrival in Transnistria, Jews between the age of 16-60 (mostly men but often also women) had to carry out various tasks under the directives of the authorities. On numerous occasions children under the age of 12 and old people over 70 were forced to work. In the beginning, workers were collected at random. Gendarmes and soldiers caught people in the streets or pulled them out of houses, and ordered them to labor units. Later, Jewish offices were set up everywhere for the purpose of organizing work; these brought some semblance of order to the chaos, especially in deciding exactly who was suitable or not suitable for certain jobs, or by laying down guidelines as to who should do what.   /.../

August 19, 1942

Under the request of the Todt-organization, Colonel Loghin, the Prefect of Tulcin county, handed over 3,000 Jews to the Germans. These were taken from those deported from Chernovitz in June. The Germans forced them to cross the Bug; 400 of the remaining Jews were left in the quarry, 140 in Ladijin, 78 in Oleanita and approx. 1,000 in Celvertinovca. Almost no one returned from among those handed over. The old people and a number of the women, children and the disabled were shot dead in the first days. The others were executed group by group, depending on their ability to continue working.   /.../

September 12, 1942

A train arrives in Tiraspol with Jews deported from Romania. From among them 407, accused of communist activity had been interned in the camp in Targu Jiu, 85 had been convicted for the same reason, 554 had been rounded up because they had been suspected of being communist sympathizers, and 587 had been taken because in 1940 during the Iron Guard terror they had asked for permission to emigrate into the Soviet Union.

Those in the first three categories were taken to the camp in Vapniarca. Those in the last category were taken to Mostvoi-Berezovca, where the headquarters of the Gestapo were located.   /.../

October 5, 1942

Major Orasanu, Commander of the Gendarme Legion in Moghilev, traveled to Sargorod to personally inform the leaders of the ghetto of the decree he had issued to transfer 3,300 Jews from the district to Peciora, 1,000 from Sargorod, 1,000 from Djurin and 1,000 from Murafa. After long negotiations, the Major agreed to withdraw his decree, after he received what he had been bargaining for: a one and a half carat cut diamond ring.

October 12, 1942

In Moghilev the transportation of the 3,000 Jews to the camp of Peciora begins. General Iliescu, Inspector of the Gendarmerie of Transnistria, proposes that the poorest people should be sent, because—in his opinion—they will perish anyway, and the camp in Peciora was created exclusively for this reason.

The Jewish Committee, along with the Gendarme Legion, arranges for the deportation to be executed gradually, and only one group of 500 people is to be taken away at a time.

The camp was known throughout Transnistria as a "death camp", (these words were even written on a board above the entrance to the camp). The inhabitants of the ghetto did everything to avoid deportation. They hid in cellars and holes under the ground, they escaped to meadows in the rain in order to hide in cornfields and ditches. Gendarmes searched for them with police dogs.

Eighty evacuees were packed into each freight-car. The doors and windows were kept closed for the whole journey, and the weaker ones suffocated.

People were removed from the freight-cars in Israilovca, 14 kms from Peciora. From there, they were taken to the camp on foot; gendarmes beat and tortured them throughout the journey.   /.../

March, 1943

In October 1943, Wilhelm Fischer, the Romanian representative of the World Jewish Federation, manages to contact foreign—mostly Swiss—leading Jewish circles (Dr. A. Silberstein from Geneva, representative of the World Jewish Federation, and Saly Mayer from Saint Gallen, European representative of the American Joint Distribution Committee). They provide him with a financial base, which at the moment, cannot be raised in the country. Wilhelm Fischer receives loans from a few generous men on condition that they will not be repaid until the war has ended. In this way he manages to collect 28 million lei (at that time 70,000 dollars), half of this was sent to Transnistria with special representatives as aid for the Jews there.   /.../

May 10, 1943

Six hundred people (men, women, young girls) are transferred across the Bug from the camp in Peciora.   /.../

May 26, 1943

The Leader of the State orders the deportation to Transnistria of Dr. W. Filderman, ex-President of the Union of Jewish Religious Communities, because he handed in a report to the President of the Central Jewish Office, in which he expressed his opinion that the Jewish population would be unable to pay the most recent 4 million lei special contribution levied on them.   /.../

May 30, 1943

In Mostovoi there are mass-executions throughout the entire month of May. The victims are selected under the pretext that they have been chosen for work. They are executed in various places near Mostovoi, mostly in Vasilinovo. Before being executed they are tortured terribly. Several are viciously murdered. The mayor of the ghetto, who had come from Chernovitz, was cut into pieces, because he had not provided young girls to perform sexual acts. An engineer from Chernovitz, who protected his wife when policemen wanted to rape her, was also cut into pieces, but first he was forced to watch the mutilation of his wife before his eyes. /.../

October 20, 1943

The Jews suffering in the camp of Slivina were handed over to the Germans, who executed the majority of them. The few who managed to avoid death, arrived in Grosolovo in terrible condition. /.../

December 10, 1943

In one day, Germans murder the remaining 438 survivors from the camp in Tarasivca, beyond the Bug, and throw their corpses into a hole. Almost all of them had been deported from Chernovitz and Dorohoi in June 1942.

The 350 Jews, still alive in Ovadovca, Talalevca and Crasnopolca, meet the same fate. They are the last to be executed from the 3,000 Jews deported to sites near Ladijin. They had been given as a present to the Todt unit in August 1942 by Colonel Loghin, the Prefect of Tulcin county, and were taken eastwards from the middle of the Bug.

January 1, 1944

Ion Antonescu cynically claims in his new year speech addressed to the army that no one had been deported and the Romanian army had been passive and tolerant.

February 5, 1944

The Pope sends 1,350,000 lei in aid to Transnistrian Jews to the Central Jewish Office through the Romanian Foreign Ministry.

March 20, 1944

In the final weeks of fascist rule Jewish deportees were not tortured in the way they had been throughout the previous three years. They were no longer beaten by officers and soldiers, and neither were they attacked by police superintendents, pharmacists or forestry engineers. They were not forced to work, nor were they transported. The "bloody Jews" had become "Jewish gentlemen".

In spite of all this, Jews were full of well-founded fear and worry. They were afraid of the massacres and killings which could follow in the wake of withdrawing German troops.

The lightning Soviet attack, however, proved an obstacle to the last crimes. /.../

Repatriation

The Chronological Order of Events

November 1942- March 1944

November 12, 1944

The governmental commissioner responsible for handling the Jewish issue, Radu Lecca, held a discussion with the leaders of the Central Jewish Office. Dr. W. Filderman, former President of the Union of Jewish Religious Communities (he had been removed from the Jewish leadership by Antonescu a year previously), also participated. Radu Lecca stated the government's proposal: the emigration of 75,000 Jews would be allowed (those who had survived in Transnistria), if several tens of billions of lei were paid in return; the sum was expected to be raised by foreign Jews. Dr. Filderman asked for the negotiations to be postponed until all the Jews had been allowed home.

January 2, 1943

The government's proposal, that all the Jews would be released on the condition that their freedom was paid for in cash, and that they were to emigrate immediately on arriving home, was not followed by concrete steps, but at least it served to raise the idea of their eventual return. At that time, the case of the approx. 5,000 orphans, whose lives were in danger as a consequence of the miserable conditions in Transnistria, was the most alarming. The Jewish leadership, which operated under cover, sent a petition to the government, in which they asked for the repatriation of the orphans. The issue of Jews born in the Old Kingdom who were either subsequently deported for labor service contravention; or evacuated from Dorohoi county, or those who had been taken away the previous year, because they had wanted to emigrate to the Soviet Union, was also raised.

January 9, 1944

The Romanian government linked any homecoming from Transnistria to the condition of immediate emigration, this even included the orphans. According to the government, Jews would be allowed to return home (...) only if the Gestapo permitted them to do so. The secretly working Jewish leadership contacted Dr. A. Tester, a friend of Killinger. Killinger, together with Radu Lecca, undertook the task of paving the way for the repatriation. Naturally, their good intentions cost a royal fortune. They turned to foreign Jewish organizations in an effort to cover the expenses.

January 19, 1943

In accordance with Directive No.55347, issued by the Ministry of the Interior, an instruction was given to set up a committee with the task of selecting Jews who had been "unjustly" deported to Transnistria, and interned in the camp in Vapniarca. These were to be given permission to return home.

January 25, 1943

Constantin Bursan, a lawyer, and former minister, was sent to Istanbul by the Jewish leadership, who worked under cover, to inform foreign Jewish organizations. /..../

March 1, 1943

The Jewish Agency for Palestine, through its representatives in Istanbul, assessed the issue of Romanian Jews, raised by Constantin Bursan. The Jewish leadership was promised political and financial support for the plan aimed at repatriating Jews and assisting their emigration.   /..../

March 17, 1943

The selection committee finished its activities in Vapniarca, after establishing that 427 of the 554 internees had been "unjustly" interned.

The committee proposed allowing them out of the camp, but keeping them in the ghettos of Transnistria. /..../

April 22, 1943

Ion Antonescu ordered that permission to return to the country was not to be given to one single Jew. General C. Z.Vasiliu, Deputy State Secretary of Police, informed the special inter-ministerial committee, which dealt with formulating regulations concerning Jews, of this decision. /..../

August 1943

When W. Filderman, the real leader of Romanian Jews, had returned from Transnistria, he sent a petition to the government, and supported it with documents). He emphasized the necessity of allowing the repatriation of all Jews, especially the orphans, and those born in Dorohoi county. /..../

October 12, 1943

Doctor W. Filderman sent the government another petition asking them to allow deported Jews to return home.

November 10, 1943

The Deputy State Secretary of the Ministry of the Interior compiled a report, in which he proposed giving permission to a number of deported Jews to return home so that they could be used as workers where the war necessitated it. /..../

December 8, 1943

Permission was given to 6,430 Jews from Dorohoi county to return home from Transnistria, and to another 218, who were interned in the camp of Vapniarca. At this time, permission to return home was also given to the 16 Jewish survivors from of the group of 568 who had been deported in autumn 1942 for applying for Soviet entry visas.

December 20, 1943

The first group of 1,500 Jews deported from Dorohoi county left Transnistria at Moghilau-Atachi. The Aid Committee provided some people with clothing. Everybody was given a train ticket and enough food to see them through a few days. However, they had to suffer until the very last minute. In some places they were harassed by Chiefs of Police and Gendarmes, who declared that the Jews were unable to conclusively prove that they had been born in Dorohoi county. (Only after acquiring a gold watch, did Colonel Gavat give permission to continue to a group of 25 people from Dorohoi). /..../

January 20, 1944

Ion Antonescu prevented the repatriation of Jews with the excuse that there were one million Romanians in Transnistria, Bessarabia and Bucovina who wanted to enter the country. If the Jews were given refuge - he declared - it would cause massive discontent. /..../

March 6, 1944

Orphans, (1,846 of them) were repatriated, 1,400 crossed the Dniester at Moghilev-Atachi, and 446 at Tiraspol-Tighina. Both groups met in Iasi, where they were distributed among the Jewish Religious Communities of Moldova and Wallachia.

March 14, 1944

/..../ Soviet troops arrived at the Bug. The radio stations of the Allies broadcast constant threats against those who had committed crimes against humanity. Ion Antonescu finally made up his mind, and decided to give an order allowing for the repatriation of all Jews deported to Transnistria.

Jewish committees immediately left for Moghilev and Tiraspol to organize the homecoming. But it was too late.

The committee which had set off for Moghilev only managed to reach Atachi, because the Soviet troops reached the Dniester on March 20, and reoccupied the entire northern region of Transnistria.

The committee which was on its way to Tiraspol got as far as Balti, where, in the southern part of the province, 2,518 deported were found, 563 of whom were taken back to the country. Most were allowed to return home, but the 563 who had been interned in Vapniarca, and taken out of the camp in Grusolovo were directed to the camp in Targu Jiu, and escorted by armed troops. /..../

Selected Documents

1.

Circular No.206798, issued by the General Headquarters of the IV Army on June 30, 1941.

We hereby notify you that under Directive No.193941 issued by the General Command we have been informed that:

Agents of the enemy are operating behind the front line. They are attempting to carry out acts of sabotage; they gather information for the enemy, and are not afraid to commit acts of violence, even against individual soldiers.

Jewish residents participate in these actions.

General Antonescu, during his visit to the front, called the attention of the commanders of the larger divisions within the army to the necessity of greater vigilance, and gave an order for the immediate execution of anyone whose actions are in any way contrary to the interests of the army or the state.

We ask you to instruct all the commanders and their divisions to take strict measures against all those found guilty of sabotage, espionage, disturbances, or any activity against the army or the state.

***

2.

Telephone report No.80, August 13, 1941.

Recorded by the Gendarmerie at Kishinev under No.359 on August 13, 1941.

We inform you that on August 12, 1941 at 12.00 hrs, the military tribunal sentenced to death four terrorists who were captured in the town of Orhe by the Gendarme Legion of the town on July 21, 1941: Anatolie Romantienco, alias Alexandru the engineer, Vasile Safcu , alias official Locea, Iacob Mendel Froim , alias

Marin the teacher, and Grigore Zadov, alias Iasu the barber. We
had informed you of these people in report No.39 of August 3,
1941.

Jews in the Tatarasi-Chilia camp were shot dead, because when
they were taken to do agricultural work they refused, and behaved aggressively.

At approx. 18.00 hrs on August 6 of this year Gendarmes from
Police Squadron No.23 shot 200 Jews, and threw their corpses
into the Dniester. /..../

Colonel Meculescu m. p.

***

3.

Minutes

Recorded August 9, 1941

I, the undersigned, Heinrich Frohlich, Untersturmfuhrer, (...) presented myself at the camp in Tatareti village, where there are 451
Jews, under the command of Gh. Ioan Vetu, Captain of the Gendarmerie Legion in Chilia Noua. I handed over the written command of General Antonescu, which stated that the Jews were to
be executed immediately. /..../

Untersturmfuhrer Frolich   Captain Ioan Gh. Vetu

***

4.

An extract from a speech by Mihai Antonescu, delivered at a
meeting held on July 3, 1941 at the Ministry of the Interior: /..../

Ethnic cleansing will be carried out through means of internment
in labor camps and other such places. Jews and other aliens ex-
hibiting signs of suspicious behavior will be interned to prevent
them from harmfully influencing the people.

9.

July 5, 1942, No.192   The Office of the County

Head of Moghilev County

Confidential

To the Police Stations, Gendarme Legions and Mayor's Offices of
the county.

The issue of Jews in Moghilev county should be addressed as I
have ordered. I will not tolerate any diversion from the given instructions.

You are obliged to replace Jews working in companies with
Ukrainian experts and workers, even if these need to be brought
from other towns and villages.

We must not allow the Jews to take root in our factories.

Even if we had needed Jewish experts at the start of production,
there is no longer a justification to keep them on, when we can
substitute them.

We shall live together with the Ukrainians here, not with the
Jews. /..../

It is part of Romanian national dignity to expel Jews from all
places where they feel indispensable.

Colonel Nasturas, County Head

***

10.

A extract from the New Year's Eve speech of Ion Antonescu,
given to the army (January 1, 1942)

Dear Soldiers,

You can carry out your duties with your heads held high; and you
should not fear the day of judgement, when it comes, as it will for
all of us.

Your struggle is just.

You have behaved with modesty and humanity in the occupied territories and wherever you have been.

No one was robbed and insulted in the areas through which you marched.

Human beings are human beings to us, regardless of their nationality, and regardless of the harm they have done to us.

We have helped and supported everyone we have come across, and we have regarded them as human beings. /..../

We have not deported anyone, and you have not thrust a dagger into the chest of anybody. We have not imprisoned innocent people. We have shown respect for all beliefs and political convictions. We have not displaced either individuals or families from their homes for political or national interest. /..../

Marshal Antonescu

***

11.

The response of Marshal Antonescu to architect Clejan, who petitioned him in the interest of deported Jews:

The Leader of the Romanian State, Bucharest February 4, 1944

Mr Clejan,

Your letter referring to the situation of Jews in Transnistria and beyond the Bug, and to the sums which have to be paid for exemption from forced labor gives me an opportunity to point out some aspects concerning the issue of Romanian Jews, within the framework defined by the state of war and the events which preceded it.

As I have already explained to you in person, I was forced to deport Jews from Bessarabia and Bucovina, since the inhabitants hated them so much for their behavior during the Russian occupation of these Romanian territories. If I had not taken these ac-